Pivot-Driven
Devotionals

Bible Selections to Move You Closer to Jesus

Arnie Cole
&
W. Terry Whalin

Lincoln, Nebraska

Copyright © 2025 Arnie Cole

All rights reserved.
No part of this publication may be reproduced, distributed, or transmitted in any form or by any means, including photocopying, recording, or other electronic or mechanical methods, without the prior written permission of the publisher, except in the case of brief quotations embodied in critical reviews and certain other noncommercial uses permitted by copyright law. For permission requests, write to the publisher, addressed "Attention: Permissions Coordinator," at the address below.

Unless otherwise noted, all Scripture passages come from the New International Version Scriptures taken from the Holy Bible, New International Version®, ®. Copyright © 1973, 1978, 1984, 2011 by Biblica, Inc.™ Used by permission of Zondervan.

For bulk orders, please contact:

Back to the Bible
6400 Cornhusker Hwy Suite 100
Lincoln NE 68507
402-464-7200

Cover Design: Exuberance
Editor: Ben Zuehlke
Interior Book Design: Greg Johnson

Arnie Cole; 1950

ISBN: 979-8-9922232-0-0

Printed in the United States of America

First Printing

Start Your Pivoting Journey Here . . .

There are two things I love about having faith in Christ. First, realizing that even though Jesus intimately knows our often stumbling journey through life, He is patient and loving with us every step of the way. Second, He never gives up on us! As we grow in our Christian faith from believing that life is all about us to understanding our calling is to participate in the building of the Kingdom, Jesus patiently walks with us and guides us every step of the way. And what an incredibly joyful and fulfilling journey it is!

In my work at Back to the Bible, I hear stories all of the time of people who finally "get" these two facts.

Ray had been a Christian nearly his whole adult life. He lived, he worked, he raised a family . . . he did all of the things a Jesus believing man is expected to do in life. But by age 52, he was frustrated and a bit dejected. "Arnie, I've never led anyone to Christ. Besides doing a pretty average job with my kids' faith, I've never really discipled someone. As my hair gets grayer and thinner, I notice that my life clock is ticking downward. I'm wondering if God will ever use me in someone's life in a more substantial way. With my kids grown and out of the house, I think I'm ready."

I hear this story on a weekly basis in some form another.

Do you ever wonder if your life will make a difference to another person?

It's easy, even natural, to live your life tending to number one. Our culture tells us every day how to live a happy and productive life. We're told to get an education, start a family, save for retirement etc.

And while there's nothing wrong with many of the things our culture prescribes, it misses a deeper, more essential point. True purpose is only found in a relationship with Jesus Christ. For many decades of my own life, I pursued the worldly goals of success. But then God got ahold of my heart, and I pivoted to a life of faith in Him. I haven't been the same since.

As a research scientist by trade, I've spent the last several decades surveying Christ followers. And we've discovered that most Christians are what we would call "notional" Christians. They know the facts, but they're not doing anything to share their faith with others. But it's not too late. As a result, they miss out on all the rich spiritual blessings that come from closely following Jesus and are left no better than those who don't know Jesus at all.

Whether you're a young adult or eighty years of age, it's not too late to consider a pivot.

Pivot toward serving the souls around you and deepening your relationship with them and God.

Pivot toward a faith strong enough—and ready enough—to answer the questions of those seeking God.

Pivot toward loving those that Jesus loved.

The Bible is full of stories of pivots. Moments of decisions where a crucial decision, or a step of faith transformed a person's life forever. Sometimes these pivots are seen in dramatic acts faith like when Abraham followed God's call to the Promised Land. Other times, a pivot is seen in the quiet assurance of faith like Simeon had as he patiently awaited the day he would see the Savior, refusing to give up hope.

Do you need to make a pivot?

I wrote this book to help you see that it's never too late to make a pivot. Each short devotional centers on a story about a biblical character or set of characters. Then I'll provide a challenge to you, pinpointing one area you can **pivot from** and then a place you can **pivot to.** And then you'll find a **prayer** and a **call to action** to take with you as you go about your day.

My prayer for you is that you will see and be motivated to start, continue, or increase your desire to become more than a notional Christian. I pray that by keeping focused on building God's Kingdom you'll see what abundant living is all about.

Arnie Cole, Winter 2025

Manasseh: His Lifelong Search

"Train up a child in the way he should go, and when he is old he will not depart from it."
(Proverbs 22:6, NKJV)

Will a son always follow in the footsteps of his father? According to 2 Chronicles, when Hezekiah became king at 25 years old, he purified the temple and called the Israelites to celebrate the Passover. "This was the largest crowd of people that had ever celebrated Passover, according to the official records." 2 Chronicles 30:5b (CEV). Hezekiah followed the Lord God with all his heart and throughout his life.

When King Hezekiah died, his oldest son, Manasseh, age 12, became king for the next 55 years (2 Chronicles 33:1). His actions turned the people in the opposite direction. "He did evil in the eyes of the LORD, following the detestable practices of the nations the LORD had driven out before the Israelites" (2 Chronicles 33:2). Instead of following the Scripture, Manasseh turned to witchcraft, sorcery, and divination. He even sacrificed his sons in the fire to the pagan god Molech. This king desecrated the temple, promoted idolatry throughout the kingdom and built many different types of pagan shrines and temples. There is an old tradition in Judaism that Manasseh executed the prophet, Isaiah.

Ultimately the Babylonians attacked Judah and took King Manasseh to Babylon bound in bronze shackles (2 Chronicles 33:11). His life was rooted in a spiritual search for truth and while in a Babylonian prison, Manasseh humbled himself and turned to the Lord his God. "And when he prayed to him, the LORD was moved by his entreaty and listened to his plea; so he brought him back to Jerusalem and to his kingdom" (2 Chronicles 33:13). A transformed man, King Manasseh threw out the pagan gods and rebuilt the Lord's temple and altar. God's Word reveals Manasseh's repentance was a complete transformation with a sincere humility and reverence for the Lord.

Maybe you have a child or a relative or a co-worker who has made some radical spiritual choices leading them away from the living God. On the surface, this person has no spiritual leanings, and it appears as though their life is headed on a path of destruction, away from following the ways of the Lord. While these life choices and actions are significant, people sometimes continue for years in the wrong spiritual direction. As a friend or parent, it feels like your prayers are not getting past the ceiling. Yet you can gain hope and insight from the story of Manasseh. Even the evilest king can repent, change and turn to the Lord God. His changed life reveals the depth of God's mercy and his long-suffering patience and grace. Continue praying for this person whose life needs to go in the Lord's direction and then trust God's guidance for their life.

Pivot from ever giving up that you don't have a role to play in someone else's spiritual journey.

Pivot to a life that appreciates everyone's spiritual journey, and realize you have a small role to play in God's big plan for those who come into your life, especially your own family and church family.

Prayer
"Lord, in Your wisdom, You know the person that I'm thinking about and the spiritual direction of their life. Thank You that Your plans and ways are beyond what I can see or imagine. In the name of Jesus, amen."

Your Pivotal Moment of Faith
At the end of this book, or on a blank sheet of paper, make a list of several people in your life who are not Christians but need God's touch in their lives. Commit to pray for them on a consistent basis.

Zacchaeus: A Life Transformed

"The LORD does not look at the things people look at. People look at the outward appearance, but the LORD looks at the heart." (1 Samuel 16:7b)

When Jesus lived in Israel, a single occupation was among the most hated among the Jewish people: the tax collector. The Roman government had placed a strict tax on the population and used these tax collectors to enforce their laws. Not all of these collectors were equal in their roles. One was known as "The Chief Tax Collector," his name was Zacchaeus, and he was a man of short height The Gospel of Luke tells us he was wealthy and had apparently cheated many fellow Israelites to become that way. (Luke 19:2,8). Everyone in the city of Jericho knew Jesus Christ was coming and they had heard the stories of His teaching and how He healed the sick. Zacchaeus wanted to see this man for himself; the one they called "the Messiah."

As crowds of people lined the street, short Zacchaeus could tell he would never be able to push through them and see Jesus. He decided to run ahead of the gathering crowd where he saw a sycamore tree beside the road. When he reached the tree, he pulled up through the branches and located a perch above the road. He was in a perfect location to have a good look at this man called Jesus. In the distance, he could hear the rumble and shout of the crowd. Jesus was coming straight toward him.

"When Jesus reached the spot, he looked up and said to him, 'Zacchaeus, come down immediately. I must stay at your house today'" (Luke 19:5). From reading Luke's Gospel, we don't know how Jesus knew the man's name. But right away the tax collector climbed down from the tree and welcomed Jesus into his home.

The crowd did not expect Jesus to speak with Zacchaeus. In fact, the people complained that Jesus was going into a sinner's home. Jesus gave Zacchaeus a chance and because He did, Zacchaeus changed his life. He declared he would give half his possessions to the poor and if he had cheated anyone, he would pay them four times the amount. Jesus proclaimed salvation had come to Zacchaeus. Jesus explained that His mission was to seek and save the lost. Jesus saw the heart of this tax collector which was nothing that man could see from the outside.

It takes spiritual maturity and a sensitivity to God's Spirit to see other people as God sees them. As Christians we need to look beyond the surface and ask the Lord to show us their heart. This depth of knowing someone else takes time but can be the pivot point leading to a radical transformation for another person like Zacchaeus.

Pivot from not seeing how unique and special each person is to God.

Pivot to becoming a "noticer" of how people need a touch from God through your genuine concern, your words of affirmation and love, and your desire to never give up on anyone.

Prayer

"Lord Jesus, help me to have new eyes to see the people You put into my life, and value them as you do. Show me how to think about them and love them as You love them. In Jesus' name."

Your Pivotal Moment of Faith

Have you had a genuine encounter with Jesus that has changed your life in some way? Write down this short story or testimony and make a point to tell it to at least one other person over the next couple of weeks.

Naaman: From Arrogance to Humility

"By humility and the fear of the LORD are riches and honor and life." (Proverbs 22:4, NKJV)

In ancient times, leprosy was one of the worst diseases a person could have, and it was incurable. Second Kings 5 tells the story of Naaman, a great and highly respected commander of the Syrian army. Known as a man with tremendous courage, Naaman was also a leper. In one of their raids, the Syrians had captured a young Israelite girl who served Naaman's wife. One day, this servant said to her mistress, "I wish Naaman would go and see the prophet in Israel who would heal his leprosy."

Eager to be healed, Naaman spoke to his king and requested permission to see the prophet. His king said, "Go to Israel and I will send a letter with you to the king of Israel."

When King Jehoram of Israel received this letter, he tore his clothing in distress and outrage saying, "I am not God to heal this man of leprosy." News of King Jehoram's reaction and response spread throughout Israel.

When Elisha the prophet heard about King Jehoram's reaction, he sent a message to the king saying, "Send Naaman to me, and he will learn that there is a true prophet here in Israel" (2 King 5:8, NLT). With great fanfare and hope, this commander went to the prophet. Instead of meeting with him, Elisha sent a simple message, "Go wash in the Jordan River seven times and your leprosy will disappear."

Naaman was furious and disappointed with the prophet's message. Elisha didn't even make the effort to meet with him in person but sent a messenger. Naaman's servants cautioned their master, "If Elisha had asked you to do something complicated, wouldn't you have done it? Why don't you follow the prophet's instructions and wash seven times in the Jordan River to see if it works?"

Naaman finally agreed and washed seven times in the Jordan. As he came out of the water for the final time, the leprosy on his skin disappeared and he was instantly cured. In that moment, Naaman's attitude changed from arrogance and disbelief to humility combined with a passionate belief in the God of Israel. As he told Elisha, "Behold, I know that there is no God in all the earth, except in Israel" (2 Kings 5:15, AMP).

Naaman's story teaches us our obedience to the ways of the Lord doesn't have to be complicated. Instead, the Lord wants us to have a steadfast love for others and trust Him in all matters, big or small. As we consistently read the Scriptures and follow God's leading in our lives, we will be blessed as we trust in His guidance instead of our own.

Pivot from skepticism about your ability to help others.

Pivot to the sure knowledge that a more simple and doable faith is one that prioritizes people and the well-being of their souls.

Prayer
"God, help me to resist excessive reasoning like Naaman's first response and instead, be led by Your Spirit—even when it doesn't make sense to my natural mind. In Jesus' name."

Your Pivotal Moment of Faith
Is there a situation in your life where you have overthought and excessively reasoned? Pause and commit it to God and humbly ask the Spirit for His guidance and leading like He led Naaman.

Euodia and Syntyche: Pivot from Disagreement to Unity

"If it is possible, as far as it depends on you, live at peace with everyone." (Romans 12:18)

When you read about the early Christians in Acts 2:42-47, the believers appear unified. We learn the believers were all together and had everything in common (verse 44). Every day they continued to meet together in the temple courts and fellowshipped as they ate together in their homes (verse 45).

Yet like today's Christians, everything wasn't perfect among those believers. In his letter to the church at Philippi, the Apostle Paul reveals some reality. In Philippians 4:2-3, Paul calls out two women leaders, Euodia and Syntyche, who were having a disagreement. These two verses don't give any details about their conflict, but it was clearly undermining church life. The church met in houses and some commentators speculated that perhaps the church met in each of their houses and they developed a competition between them. It would not be unusual for Euodia and Syntyche to have important roles as women in the church because Philippi was the leading city in Macedonia and Macedonian women enjoyed greater freedom and rights than other women during this time.

Whatever the reason for the disagreement, it could not have run too deep because Paul believed both of their names were "in the Book of Life" (Philippians 4:3). Instead, the Apostle encouraged the women to seek the mind of Christ and not their own direction. Paul faced head-on the division between these two Christian women. Just a little later in Philippians, Paul gives the early Christians the prescription for victory over worry saying, "Be anxious for nothing, but in everything by prayer and supplication, with thanksgiving, let your requests be known to God; and the peace of God, which surpasses all understanding, will guard your hearts and minds through Christ Jesus" (Philippians 4:6-7, NKJV).

How can you make the change from a disagreement to unity?

Jesus knew there would be disagreements, even among Christians, and He gave us the pattern on how to handle disagreements. Matthew 18:15 says, "If another believer sins against you, go privately and point out the offense. If the other person listens and confesses it, you have won that person back" (NLT). Notice you don't confront someone in public but in private. When you have a conflict, it takes courage to reach out to the other person and resolve it.

Think of when you had a disagreement with a family member or neighbor or another Christian. How did you handle it? What lessons can you learn for handling disagreements in the future?

Pivot from the need to always win arguments or feel superior to others.

Pivot to seeing people and situations the way Jesus might see them, realizing everyone has a story that has led them to weak moments when they're not the person or Christian they wish they could be.

Prayer
"Heavenly Father, give me Your wisdom and insight about how to resolve any disagreement with another person and to live in peace. Show me how to change and what I should say. In Jesus' name."

Your Pivotal Moment of Faith
Recall a disagreement in your life with a relative or a friend. How did you resolve it? What can you learn from the Scriptures about the actions to take in the future in order to live in peace?

Mary: Embracing a Simple Faith

"My soul glorifies the Lord and my spirit rejoices in God my Savior." (Luke 1:46b-47)

The experience would shock anyone. Mary, a teenager, was engaged to be married to Joseph, a carpenter in Nazareth. Suddenly, the Angel Gabriel appeared to her. "The angel went to her and said, 'Greetings, you who are highly favored! The Lord is with you.'" (Luke 1:28) For most people, the appearance of an angel would have shocked them, and Mary was no different. The Bible describes Mary as "greatly troubled." She wondered about the meaning of such a greeting. Gabriel continued and told her that she would bear a son and she was to name Him Jesus, and He would sit on the throne of King David, and His reign would never end. As a young virgin who was only engaged, Mary asked the angel how such a thing was possible.

Gabriel answered, "'The Holy Spirit will come on you, and the power of the Most High will overshadow you. So the holy one to be born will be called the Son of God'" (Luke 1:35). Then the angel included some additional insight about Mary's relative Elizabeth. "Even Elizabeth your relative is going to have a child in her old age, and she who was said to be unable to conceive is in her sixth month. For no word from God will ever fail'" (Luke 1:36-37).

Instead of running or doubting or protesting, Mary did none of these actions. Instead, she turned and responded to the call of God with humility and simple faith. "'I am the Lord's servant,' Mary answered. 'May your word to me be fulfilled'" (Luke 1:38). As a virgin, Mary faced the pressure and judgement of society when she made this pivotal response. The angel's news transformed her ordinary life into becoming the mother of Jesus, the Son of God and Savoir of the world. Her calling was a fulfillment of a prophecy spoken by the prophet Isaiah who said the Messiah would be born of a virgin (Isaiah 7:14).

Throughout the centuries, Mary, the mother of Jesus, has become a model of simple obedience and faithful action to her calling. As you read the stories like this one in the Bible, God can use them to direct your steps, but only if you are listening and committed to taking action. The first step in the process is to be sensitive to God's direction and His Spirit as you read the Scripture. More than listening, you also need to take action as God directs your steps. What can you learn from the actions of Mary?

Pivot from a faith that doesn't listen to the still, small voice.

Pivot to a more simple and obedient faith, realizing that our obedience is to the command to love God and love our neighbor as ourselves.

Prayer

"Lord, thank You for the example of Mary and her simple faith and trust in Your guidance in her life. Help me to learn from her example in my own life. In the name of Jesus."

Your Pivotal Moment of Faith

God can only direct our steps if we are listening to His Spirit through prayer and a consistent reading of Scripture. As we hear His guidance, then we need to take action on His directions. What steps can you take in your life to move more in this direction?

Elijah: Facing Burnout

"'Come to me, all you who are weary and burdened, and I will give you rest. Take my yoke upon you and learn from me, for I am gentle and humble in heart, and you will find rest for your souls.'" (Matthew 11:28-29)

A lengthy drought had ravaged the land of Israel. Then "the word of the LORD came to Elijah: 'Go and present yourself to Ahab, and I will send rain on the land'" (1 Kings 18:1b). The prophet Elijah proposed a contest on Mount Carmel between himself and the 450 false prophets of Baal. Each group would prepare a single sacrifice with wood and the animal. Two oxen were prepared, and Elijah had the prophets of Baal select their oxen and he took the other one. Neither one would use fire with their sacrifice. "'Then you call on the name of your god, and I will call on the name of the LORD. The god who answers by fire—he is God.' Then all the people said, 'What you say is good'" (1 Kings 18:24).

Elijah suggested the Baal prophets go first since there were so many of them. The Baal prophets shouted from morning until noon. When nothing happened, Elijah mocked them saying, "Maybe your god is busy or asleep. Cry louder to get his attention." These Baal prophets even took knives and cut themselves trying to get the attention and fire from their god. After a lot of commotion with no fire for their sacrifice, they gave up.

Now Elijah took his turn. First, he rebuilt the Lord's altar using twelve stones to represent the twelve tribes of Israel. Then he prepared his sacrifice, cutting the animal and placing the wood around it. Next the prophet filled four pitchers with water and poured it over the sacrifice. Then he filled those pitchers a second time and the water filled a ditch around the altar. Finally, everything was prepared. Elijah uttered a short, simple prayer and fire came down from heaven. In that moment the people realized the True God of Israel was with Elijah and they gathered all the prophets of Baal and slaughtered them.

King Ahab returned to his palace where he told his wife, Queen Jezebel, about the contest and the death of the false prophets of Baal. Queen Jezebel vowed to kill the prophet, Elijah. In fear for his life, the prophet ran and hid under a broom tree in the desert. After such a huge spiritual victory, Elijah experienced a physical burnout. Over several days the Angel of the Lord came and fed him to restore his strength.

Life as a Christian is full of surprises and challenges. These surprises or challenges often require vast amounts of personal energy. Recall a time when you have experienced a success at work or a victory with your family after an intense situation. Like the prophet Elijah, you will often need to take time to rest and recover or you will burn out. To handle the highs and lows of life, each of us needs to find balance as a critical element.

Pivot from not taking time to rejuvenate your body and spirit after stressful days or seasons.

Pivot to a life of balance, consistent battery recharging, and quiet moments with the Lord where you renew your strength.

Prayer
"Lord, thank You that Your presence is in my life whether I succeed or fail. Through Your Holy Spirit, give me the balance that I need day by day. In Jesus' name."

Your Pivotal Moment of Faith
What life lessons can you learn from the prophet Elijah as you handle the highs and lows of your daily life? Make some notes here or in your journal so you can remember to balance actions with rest.

Moses: Continually Curious

"Show me your ways, O LORD; teach me your paths." (Psalm 25:4, NKJV)

The sheep were scattered on the far side of the desert and near the mountain of God. Moses was shepherding the flock of his father-in-law Jethro.

When he was a baby, Moses, a Hebrew, was raised by Pharoah's daughter in the royal family of Egypt. Moses was aware of the harsh way the Egyptians treated his fellow Jewish people. One day he saw an Egyptian beating one of his Hebrew countrymen. Looking around and seeing no one, Moses killed the Egyptian and hid the body. The next day, he saw two Hebrews fighting and intervened. They asked, "Are you going to kill one of us as you did the Egyptian?" Moses knew his secret was out and that Pharoah would eventually try to kill him. He fled to the Midian desert. There, he helped some women water their flocks. The woman's father, Jethro, invited Moses to work with him and care for his flocks.

Now the former prince spent his days in the desert caring for the sheep. From time to time, Moses moved the sheep to a new area of the desert to graze. He was keenly aware of his environment as he watched over the flocks. One day, a strange sight in the distance caught his attention. A burning bush. But what was keeping it on fire but not consuming the bush? Always curious about something new, Moses walked closer to the burning bush. He thought to himself, "'I will go over and see this strange sight—why the bush does not burn up'" (Exodus 3:3). As he approached the burning bush, he heard his name. God was calling him from within the burning flames, "Moses, Moses!" How in the world did a burning bush know his name?

At the sound of his name a second time, Moses simply answered, "Here I am."

From within the bush, God spoke, "'Do not come any closer . . . Take off your sandals, for the place where you are standing is holy ground" (Exodus 3:5). Because of his curiosity about a burning bush, Moses investigated, and God called his name. The conversation changed the direction of his life. God gave Moses a mission which moved him forever from herding sheep in the desert. Instead, God directed Moses to lead his people out of Egypt and into the Promised Land.

The old saying goes, the journey of a thousand miles begins with a single step . . . or a single act of curiosity. God can direct the steps of our lives but only if we are sensitive to the leading of His Spirit and listening to His voice through reading Scripture.

Pivot from a life where you think your best days are behind you.

Pivot to a life of Kingdom purpose where your future direction comes from the Lord.

Prayer

"Lord, thank You for the curiosity of Moses and how You directed his steps through the burning bush. Guide me continually, direct my steps, and help me to study and learn from the stories in the Bible. In the name of Jesus."

Your Pivotal Moment of Faith

Grow your curiosity about the world around you and commit to spending more time on quiet moments of reflection, as well as contemplating God's Word on a consistent basis.

David: Faith to Expand His Experience

"You are my hiding place; you will protect me from trouble and surround me with songs of deliverance." (Psalm 32:7)

For forty days, the nine-foot-tall Philistine Goliath came out every day and taunted King Saul and the Israelite army. Instead of the armies fighting each other, Goliath challenged the Israel army to send a single person to come and fight to the death. The winner would take everything. To find a soldier brave enough for the battle, King Saul offered a reward and the marriage of a daughter. None of the Israelite soldiers were willing to battle Goliath.

As the youngest son of Jesse, David wasn't with his brothers on the battlefield. Instead, he was watching the flocks of sheep for the family. For years, David had been caring for the family's sheep. When a bear or lion attacked, David killed the animal and defended the flock. When his father sent David with some food supplies, he heard about the giant's challenge. Throughout the camp, on the faces of the soldiers, David saw their fear. They were also discussing the reward for whoever stepped into the battle with the giant Goliath. Because he had experience killing wild animals to protect his sheep, David took a step of faith and decided to expand his experience and fight Goliath.

King Saul could see David's confidence and loaded him up with armor and a sword, but it was clumsy, and David decided he didn't need it. Instead, he went to the stream and gathered five smooth stones for his sling. On the next day, as he had other days, Goliath called out to the Israelites. To the giant's surprise, David stepped forward and into the battle. He swung his sling and planted a stone in the center of Goliath's forehead. Then grabbing the giant's sword, David cut off Goliath's head and won the victory.

Though you don't have a real snarling giant to face, you likely do have the occasional giant-size problem at work or in your family. When you face these challenges, do you gear up with unnecessary props to make you feel strong? Or does your faith come into play in order to trust that God is truly there fighting your battles with you? Search your past and recall incidents where the Lord faithfully guided your steps. There is a faith that leads to an uncommon courage when you've seen the Lord in action specifically for you. Your past experiences can be benchmarks and reasons to move forward to conquer the giant issues you're facing.

Pivot from the fear of giant problems that seem insurmountable.

Pivot to the realization that God has always been in the business of doing the impossible for those whose hope and whose faith is in the Lord, not in their own wisdom or strength.

Prayer

"Lord, thank You for how You have guided my path in the past. Now use those experiences to help me grow my faith and trust You for new experiences. Just like David trusted You with Goliath, I trust You to slay the giants before me. In Your name. Amen."

Your Pivotal Moment of Faith

Think about some ways God has led you in the past and celebrate your learning and progress. Now use that progress as a steppingstone of faith to expand your faith in new directions.

Samuel: When God Calls in the Night

"Call to me and I will answer you and tell you great and unsearchable things you do not know." (Jeremiah 33:3)

In the days of the judges in Israel, it was a terrible burden whenever a woman could not get pregnant and bring a child into the world. The Book of 1 Samuel tells the story of Hannah who year after year came to the temple in prayer and pled with God so she could get pregnant. She promised the Lord if she became pregnant then she would give that child to the Lord for a lifetime of service. Later that year, Hannah got pregnant and bore her son, Samuel. As promised, Hannah gave her son to Eli, the high priest in Jerusalem, as a temple assistant.

During those days, the Lord rarely spoke to anyone. But one time in the middle of the night Samuel woke up from a sound sleep hearing his name and came running to Eli, thinking it must be the priest who was calling his name.

But Eli had not called him.

After it happened a second and third time, Eli had an idea about what was happening to Samuel. He instructed the young man to make a change in his response. The priest said, "Go and lie down, and if he calls you, say, 'Speak, LORD, for your servant is listening'" (1 Samuel 3:9).

Later that night Samuel again heard the voice and responded following Eli's instructions. The

Lord told Samuel that the actions of Eli and his sons grieved Him, and that they were about to face judgment. Afterwards, Samuel told Eli everything as the priest had instructed. Eli said, "The Lord's will be done." And as Samuel grew, the Lord was with him. Samuel would become known as the final judge in Israel and the first prophet of the nation.

Through the simple action of listening to the Lord, Samuel's life was changed, and he spoke for God throughout the rest of his earthly days. Today you may not hear God's audible voice, but we can seek the Lord's guidance and direction every day through our reading of the Scriptures. The stories and the words can direct our daily lives but only if we are reading and listening on a regular basis.

Pivot from the days when you weren't attempting to hear the Lord's voice.

Pivot to the practice of quiet, of reflection, of having a desire for the volume of God's voice to increase, and the volume of the world's voice to decrease.

Prayer
"Father, thank You for the example of how You called Samuel to speak for You. Give me ears to hear and a heart to listen to Your voice and to Your Word through the Scripture. Guide my steps today. In the mighty name of Jesus, I pray."

Your Pivotal Moment of Faith

If godly parents raised you, take a note card or even a simple sheet of paper and write a thoughtful letter of gratitude and mail it to them (even if they live nearby). If you don't have this type of relative, then think of a mentor or friend who has taught you some important lessons, then write and mail the letter to them. These letters are often something the receiver will cherish and keep for years, and you can have a significant role in their lives with this written gratitude.

Rahab: Incredible Courage and Faith

"When I am afraid, I will trust in you. In God, whose word I praise, in God I trust; I will not be afraid." (Psalm 56:3-4a, CSB)

The people who lived in the military stronghold and walled city of Jericho were living in fear. The news of the massive group of Jewish people and their ability to conquer cities and kings had spread across Canaan. Rahab, a prostitute, had a chance meeting with a pair of Israelites. They asked Rahab to hide them, and she agreed to take them to her roof and cover them. With a knock on her door, the men from the King of Jericho asked if she had seen the foreigners. Instead of revealing the spies, Rahab sent these men away from her home which was right on the Jericho wall.

After the soldiers left, she spoke with the spies, "I hid you so please save my life and the life of my family" (see Joshua 2:12-13). The spies agreed and told her the family had to stay within the walls of her home. Later that night, Rahab gave the men a rope so they could climb down the wall and escape out of the city. A few days later, thousands of Israelite men showed up outside Jericho, then marched silently around the city. They repeated this action each day until the seventh day when they marched around seven times. On the final time, they shouted and with the mighty hand of

God, the walls of Jericho fell down. Only Rahab and those with her in her home were spared.

But her story didn't end there. Later in the genealogy of the New Testament, we learn Rahab married a Jewish man of the tribe of Judah. She became the great, great grandmother of King David and one of the few women in the lineage of Jesus (Matthew 1:5). In the face of fear, Rahab had a daring faith and made her decision to hide the spies. This decision changed her life and eventually the course of history.

Even as believers in Jesus, fear can fill our lives. Maybe you have started a new job, or you have decided to return to school or move to a new city. Maybe you have started a new relationship or decided to call an old friend. There are any number of other activities which can drive fear into your life. Instead of focusing on the fear, follow the example of Rahab and move forward with courage and faith.

There is a saying attributed to former First Lady Eleanor Roosevelt. She said, "Do one thing every day that scares you." Pause and think about an action that scares you and then summon the courage and faith to take a thoughtful action and move it forward.

Pivot from a life where fear hinders you from trying new things to help people.

Pivot to a life of faith and expectation that God can use you in the life of people beyond what you thought possible.

Prayer

"Father, when I am afraid, I will recall the courage and faith of Rahab and move forward with trust in you. Fill my days with courage and faith, in Jesus' name."

Your Pivotal Moment of Faith

Take a few moments and consider where fear is filling your life. In faith and with God-given courage, take action to move forward.

Daniel: Praying to God Despite a Law

"Look to the LORD and his strength; seek his face always." (1 Chronicles 16:11)

When Babylon conquered Israel, they took some of the best people back to Babylon including Daniel and three others. In the early pages of Daniel, these Israelites stood out to the king and grew in influence and status among the wise men and leaders in the nation.

In Daniel 6, we see that as Daniel was successful in his work with the King of Babylon, other leaders grew jealous of his growing relationship with the ruler. As these leaders watched Daniel, they noticed he was systematic and habitual in his prayer life. Three times a day at an open window in his home, Daniel knelt and prayed to the Lord of the Universe.

These leaders set a trap for Daniel. They encouraged the King to sign a law declaring that no one could pray to anyone except to the King. Under the law of the Medes and the Persians, once the king signed a law with his seal, it could not be revoked or changed. After the law was signed and sealed, these leaders waited and watched Daniel. Even knowing about the new law, Daniel followed his normal pattern and prayed in his open window, violating the law. These leaders caught Daniel and took him to the King for punishment.

The King could see now why the other leaders had encouraged him to sign this law, but he was stuck. He could not break his own decree, nor could he free Daniel. He had no choice but to throw Daniel into a pit with hungry lions. A stone was rolled over the entrance, and the king spent a sleepless night worried about Daniel.

The next morning, they opened the pit, and the king called out to Daniel. Immediately Daniel answered and explained that God had rescued him by shutting the mouths of the lions. When Daniel was released, the king ordered the jealous men and their families to be thrown to the lions where they were instantly killed.

Jealousy is a cancer which can destroy you. As James tells us, "For where jealousy and selfish ambition exist, there will be disorder and every vile practice" (James 3:16, ESV). If you are jealous of someone, I suggest you take an unexpected action. You can turn and do something kind or unexpected to build your relationship with that person and understand where they are in life. The simple switch will change your life, end the jealousy and build a lasting relationship.

Pivot from thoughts of jealousy toward a rival.

Pivot to a life where you can always celebrate the victories of those in your world.

Prayer
"Father, whenever I feel jealous, help me to recall Daniel and his habit of prayer, and also to take an unexpected action of kindness toward this

person to build my relationship with them. I turn to You to move in my heart and direct my steps. In Jesus' name."

Your Pivotal Moment of Faith

When others succeed it's easy to become jealous of that person. What different actions can you take to help that person and rid your life of jealousy? Write down the person's name and a sentence or two describing what actions you will take for this person.

Nicodemus: A Late Night Discovery of the Messiah

"For God so loved the world that he gave his one and only Son, that whoever believes in him shall not perish but have eternal life." (John 3:16)

How could these miracles happen in Israel? In homes and in the streets, people were discussing the miracles of Jesus Christ from Nazareth. No one had an explanation about how the blind could instantly see after only a touch. No one could explain how those with diseases were instantly healed after meeting the Nazarene. Men and women who had been crippled and couldn't walk for years were able to stand and run when Jesus spoke to them. Even among the religious leaders in the temple, they were re-telling the stories about Jesus and talking about Him. One evening, a cautious leader named Nicodemus, a Pharisee, found the courage to speak with Jesus. Approaching Jesus, he said, "Rabbi, we know that you are a teacher who has come from God. For no one could perform the signs you are doing if God were not with him" (John 3:2b).

Jesus welcomed the opportunity to talk with this leader and uttered one of the most quoted Bible verses, "Very truly I tell you, no one can see the kingdom of God unless they are born again" (John 3:3).

The words made Nicodemus wrinkle his face and say, "How can someone be born when they are old?" (John 3:4). Jesus then engaged in the conversation with more detail about His mission in the world. The words of Jesus changed Nicodemus, but the change isn't explained until later in the Gospel of John.

Jesus is nailed to a cross and dies. When they brought His body into the family tomb of Joseph of Arimathea which he had given up for Jesus, Nicodemus was also there and carried with him a mixture of myrrh and aloes, and then worked with Joseph to prepare Jesus' body for burial (John 19:39). This old Pharisee rendered a loving act to Jesus in that tomb. Of course, three days later that body was gone and the tomb empty. The Lord had risen!

Throughout the centuries, evangelists have told and retold the story of the nighttime visit of Nicodemus along with the words of John 3:16. "For God so loved the world that he gave his one and only Son, that whoever believes in him shall not perish but have eternal life.'"

Before Jesus left earth, He commissioned every Christian to spread the truth of God's Kingdom. That privilege is not just for evangelists or preachers. As believers our actions and words are a story to our neighbors and everyone who crosses our path throughout the day—either positive or negative. Maybe you frequent a morning coffee shop: can others tell by how you treat the staff that you are a Christ-follower? How about your interactions at the grocery store; at the office; watching your kids or grandkids in their sports?

Can others tell from your character and words that you are different because you follow Jesus?

Pivot from not believing your life and words could make an impact on friends or strangers around you.

Pivot to a life that notices the spark of God in every human and treats them the way Jesus would.

Prayer
"God, thank You for how You spoke and changed the life of Nicodemus. Guide my life and words so others know that I am a follower of Jesus. Give me the courage and boldness to tell others about You and how You have changed my life. In Jesus' name."

Your Pivotal Moment of Faith
Take a few moments and think about ways you represent Jesus in everyday life. Then make a fresh commitment for Jesus to fill your life and actions.

Esther: Born for Such a Time as This

"My times are in your hands; deliver me from the hands of my enemies, from those who pursue me."
(Psalm 31:15)

During the reign of King Xerxes of Persia (486-465 BC), the Jewish people were exiled from Israel and scattered across other countries. The Scriptures make it clear they were exiled because they had continually rejected God. The Book of Esther is set during King Xerxes' reign. Before Esther was born, the King of Persia had conquered Babylon, and the Persian king gave the Jews permission to return to Israel. Many of the Jews including Esther's family decided to stay in Persia.

King Xerxes threw a multi-day celebration and on the seventh day, he asked for Queen Vashti to come to him, "wearing her royal crown, in order to display her beauty to the people and nobles" (Esther 1:11) The Queen refused to come, and the King asked his wisemen what would be a proper punishment. They suggested he ban Vashti from his presence and take the crown away from her and then hold a contest to find a replacement. Esther, a Jewish woman and orphan was chosen to become the new queen.

Later, Haman, a leader in Persia, was offended by Mordecai. Mordecai, a devout Jew, and Esther's uncle, refused to bow his knee to Haman. As a result, Haman plotted to kill all of the Jews (Esther 3:5).

When Mordecai learned of this, he asked his niece to plead with the King for the lives of the Jewish people. And in his message, he said to Esther. "For if you remain silent at this time, relief and deliverance for the Jews will arise from another place, but you and your father's family will perish. And who knows but that you have come to your royal position for such a time as this?" (Esther 4:14).

Esther responded with this reply to Mordecai: "'Go, gather together all the Jews who are in Susa, and fast for me. Do not eat or drink for three days, night or day. I and my attendants will fast as you do. When this is done, I will go to the king, even though it is against the law. And if I perish, I perish" (Esther 4:16).

Miraculously, the queen was granted entrance to see the king. He could have refused but he welcomed her into his court. Esther asked the king and Haman to come to a dinner. The king and Haman ate with Queen Esther. When the king asked his queen what he could do for her, Esther asked the king and Haman to return for a second dinner. During the second dinner, Esther pleaded for the king to spare her life and the life of her people. She then detailed Haman's plot against the Jews. The king was outraged and had Haman executed. The Jewish people throughout Persia were rescued.

A key theme in this Bible story is the timing and position of Esther. She did something active for her people in order to save their lives. It's critical for any activity to include the right timing. Maybe you are seeking a new relationship or new job or a new church. Who you ask and where you search, and the timing of these open doors is an important part of the consideration process.

Pivot from the belief that God has no part in orchestrating your life events for your good.

Pivot to the firm knowledge that God is involved in the small and big events of your life in order to bless your life so you can be a blessing to others.

Prayer
Lord, help me to be aware of the importance of timing with my decisions and actions. I ask You to open doors and shut doors in my everyday life. Give me the courage and bravery of Esther as I make small but important daily decisions.

Your Pivotal Moment of Faith
Recall a period in your life where timing was an important aspect of the open door you went through.

Ruth: Loyal and Faithful

"Ruth replied, 'Don't urge me to leave you or to turn back from you. Where you go, I will go, and where you stay, I will stay. Your people will be my people and your God my God.'" (Ruth 1:16)

During the time of the judges in Israel's history three women journeyed along a dusty road heading toward Bethlehem, Judah in the nation of Israel. Years before, famine had swept across the land and Naomi, her husband Elimelech and their two sons fled to Moab and stayed there ten years. During this time away from their homeland, Elimelech died, and Naomi was left in Moab with her two sons who had married Moabite women named Orpah and Ruth. Then each of the sons died.

The news arrived in Moab that the famine had broken in Israel and once again they had food. The three women, Naomi and her two daughters-in-law, decided to travel from Moab to Bethlehem. While traveling, Naomi released Orpah and Ruth from any obligation to travel with her to Israel saying, "Go return to your mother's home and surely you will find rest in your land" (see Ruth 1:8-9). Both of the daughters-in-law wept and insisted they would return with Naomi to Israel.

Trying again, Naomi said to them, "I am too old to have another husband and more children that could be your husbands. God's hand is against me.

Return to your homeland." Once again, the two younger women wept and protested. Orpah said her good-byes and returned to her family in Moab. But Ruth made a different and pivotal decision to stay with Naomi and to go with her to Bethlehem. Ruth said, "Your people will be my people and your God my God" (Ruth 1:16b).

After this critical decision, Ruth gleaned wheat in the fields of Boaz, a kinsman of Naomi's. Ultimately, she married Boaz. We see how God blessed Ruth's decision to stick by Naomi by the fact that Ruth's name is in the lineage of Jesus (Matthew 1:3). And she was the great grandmother of David, the shepherd King.

Today you may be facing what seems like a difficult—perhaps impossible—situation . . . with a child, a job, or a relationship. On the surface it may seem like there are no good options to resolve the problem.

If you give up, you will never find the solution, but if you persist, continue praying and trusting for a solution, then God can reveal a way for it to work out. But only if you persist and do not give up. Like Ruth and Naomi, you may be in a dire circumstance which God can direct if you continue to trust Him. The answer might not come instantaneously but the Lord wants us to turn and depend on Him and His plan.

Pivot from a life of self-sufficiency with God on the side as a backup in case you can't figure something out.

Pivot to a life of dependency on God, confident in the anticipation that the God who loved and died for you is able to direct your steps while you trust in Him.

Prayer
Thank you, Father, that You are always available to direct my steps even when there are dire and difficult circumstances. Show me the way forward. In Jesus' name.

Your Pivotal Moment of Faith
Make brief notes about a situation which currently looks difficult, perhaps even dire. Reach out to a close friend for prayer and counsel to find the way forward with God's guidance.

Joseph: An Unwavering Faith in God's Plan

"He [Jesus] replied, 'If you have faith as small as a mustard seed, you can say to this mulberry tree, "Be uprooted and planted in the sea," and it will obey you.'" (Luke 17:6)

From a distance, his brothers instantly could identify Joseph because of his multi-colored coat, a gift from his father. "Here comes the dreamer," one of the brothers uttered to another. The eleventh son of his father and firstborn of his favorite wife, Rachel, Joseph knew his father, Israel (Jacob), favored him—the special coat was the proof. This favored role bothered each of his older brothers. When Joseph's brothers saw that their father loved him more than any of them, they hated him and could not speak a kind word to him.

But that wasn't all. Joseph told his brothers about a dream where they were binding grain, and the other sheaves of grain bowed down to his sheave. Days later in another dream, the sun and moon and eleven stars bowed down to Joseph. Joseph's brothers and his parents instantly knew the dream was about them. Israel kept this dream in his heart (Genesis 37:3-11).

Not long after this, when Joseph went to check on his brothers, they saw him in the distance and plotted to kill him. They dropped him into a cistern and were going to kill him . . . and then they saw the Ishmaelite merchants coming past. Instead of having the blood of their brother on their hands, they sold Joseph as a slave and his new owners took him to Egypt.

In Egypt, he lived in Potipher's house which prospered under Joseph's management until he was falsely accused of immorality and thrown into prison. While in prison, Joseph also prospered and through another dream, he came to the attention of Pharoh. In a matter of years, Joseph went from slave to second-in-command for the entire nation. In dreams, the Lord showed Joseph seven years of prosperity would be followed with seven years of famine.

During the time of famine, his brothers came to Egypt to talk with their leaders about procuring food. They met with Joseph, but they did not recognize him. It wasn't until the brothers' second trip, that Joseph revealed himself to his brothers. Though the brothers were fearful at first, the reunion was a joyful one.

Joseph's faithful following of the God of Abraham led him to forgive his brothers and to see God's guiding hand. His father Israel and the entire family moved to Egypt to be under Pharoah's and Joseph's care.

Often looking at the past will reveal God's faithful ordering of our lives and steps. Like the example of Joseph, we need to cultivate and increase our faith and trust of God's guidance in our everyday lives. If we are praying and trusting and truly relinquishing our will to the King of the Kingdom, God will guide our relationships at work and with family. He will lead our success in our job and in the church and guide what we read and who we meet—but only if we follow the journey of faith like Joseph.

Pivot from the life of faith that believes there is no room for God to do miracles.

Pivot to the joy of having the firm knowledge that God is caring and active in your everyday life so that you may continue to help people toward his Kingdom.

Prayer
"God, thank You for how You spoke to Joseph in dreams and increased his faith in his daily life. Help me to learn from this example and bring more faith into my life—even if my faith is like a tiny mustard seed."

Your Pivotal Moment of Faith
The next time you're at a garden center, buy a cheap pack of seeds and hold the actual seeds in your hand. Compare those seeds to the plant that they will eventually become. Use these seeds as a practical faith-stretching example for your own faith.

Abraham: Trusting the God of Miracles

"'For I know the plans I have for you,' declares the LORD, 'plans to prosper you and not to harm you, plans to give you hope and a future.'"
(Jeremiah 29:11)

God called Abram when he was 75 years old and living in his father's house. God said, "I will make you into a great nation, and I will bless you; I will make your name great, and you will be a blessing'" (Genesis 12:2). With faithful obedience, Abram took his wife, Sarai and his nephew Lot and they set off for the land of Canaan. Now, God had promised descendants to Abram (Genesis 15:4), but even after many years had flown by Abram and Sarai still didn't have a child. So Sarai took matters into her own hands and gave Abram her servant Hagar. Hagar bore him a son, Ishmael.

Unfortunately, Ishmael was outside of God's plan for Abram. When Abram was 99, the Lord appeared and changed Abram's name to Abraham and Sarai's name to Sarah. Again, the Lord promised Abraham a son which he had been waiting for twenty-five years. Abraham was doubtful at the idea of bearing a son at the age of 100 of a woman who was ninety. (Genesis 17:17). But God promised: "'Yes, but your wife Sarah will bear you a son, and you will call him Isaac. I will establish my covenant with him as an everlasting covenant for his descendants after him. And as for Ishmael, I have heard you: I will surely bless him; I will make him fruitful and will greatly increase his numbers. He will be the father of twelve rulers, and I will make him into a great nation. But my covenant I will establish with Isaac, whom Sarah will bear to you by this time next year'" (Genesis 17:19-21). Soon, Isaac would be born, just as the Lord promised. And from Isaac, Jacob would be born, and from Jacob, the nation of Israel. The faithful journey of Abraham shows us that God's timing isn't what man conceives.

You likely have plans for your future. Maybe it is a position with your company or a place you would like to live or a possession you would like to own. Maybe it's a goal you would like to accomplish in the coming days. As you consider the life of Abraham and his patient faith, may it teach you that God is not bound by our sense of timing. Having Kingdom faith means being confident that God's timing is perfect and beyond anything we can conceive or plan. Hebrews 11, often called the "faith chapter," includes a number of Bible characters—including Abraham—who showed great faith and trust in the Lord. These lives of these "fallible but faithful" are ones we can mirror for our own journey of faith.

Pivot from going with the flow of your own decision-making wisdom in your hope that everything will work out.

Pivot to relying on God that something bigger and better may or may not be just around the corner, but His plans for you are always perfect.

Prayer
"Lord, some days are challenging to walk by faith and not sight. Help me to follow the faithful example of Abraham in my daily life. In Jesus' name."

Your Pivotal Moment of Faith
What aspects of your life need to be changed and improved? Maybe you need a different church relationship or a different faith-full friend. Or possibly you need to increase your income and possibly change positions. What steps in faith can you take to move toward your dreams as you commit them into God's hands and guidance?

Isaiah: Radical Obedience to God

"'For God did not send his Son into the world to condemn the world, but to save the world through him.'" (John 3:17)

The nation of Israel had been divided into two kingdoms—Israel to the north and the kingdom of Judah to the south. Isaiah, the son of Amoz, was a highly educated poet who lived in Jerusalem in Judah.

In chapter six of the Book of Isaiah, he tells us of the mission he received from God. "In the year that King Uzziah died, I saw the Lord, high and exalted, seated on a throne; and the train of his robe filled the temple" (Isaiah 6:1) Isaiah could see the angels moving around the throne room of the Lord of the Universe and Isaiah shook with fear.

As he listened, the prophet could hear the holy hymn of worship flooding his ears and heart. Standing here, Isaiah felt doomed and sinful with the awareness that he was a man with unclean lips. He wondered how he could remain in the presence of a Holy God being so unclean.

Suddenly one of the seraphim lifted a burning piece of coal with tongs, then came and touched it to Isaiah's lips saying, "'Your guilt is removed, and your sins are forgiven'" (Isaiah 6:7, NLT). In an instant, he was forgiven.

Isaiah continues his account: "Then I heard the voice of the Lord saying, 'Whom shall I send? And who will go for us?' And I said, 'Here am I. Send me!' " (Isaiah 6:8). The prophet understood his people needed God's message. He committed to obey, to listen to the voice of God and deliver His words to the people.

Isaiah saw a need from the Lord and took action. Why? Because he knew God well enough to understand what was important to Him. So he listened to the Lord and responded to His instructions.

During your day, are you taking time to read and meditate on the Scriptures? Then give yourself some time to listen for the possible plan of action you can take in response to the living, breathing Word of God. Perhaps an individual will come into your mind that you haven't thought about in many months. If so, make a note to make a call today. When you do, don't be surprised if they begin by saying, "I was just thinking about you earlier today." Their reaction should bring a smile because it affirms that your actions are God-directed like in the Old Testament when the Lord directed Isaiah's actions.

Pivot from an inner life that doesn't have the goal of putting people first.

Pivot to understanding that most of responses to the nudges from Scripture will be connected to another soul who needs a touch from God—through you!

Prayer

"Father, like Isaiah, give me an awareness of my sinful nature and the forgiveness that I have through the blood of Jesus Christ. Through Your Holy Spirit, guide my actions today and use me to bring others to Jesus. In His name. Amen."

Your Pivotal Moment of Faith

Meditation on Scripture can become an important part of building or rebuilding your relationship with the Lord. Take some quiet time today and write down some spirit-directed actions.

Saul: From Simple Farmer to Ruler of a Nation

"Let everyone be subject to the governing authorities, for there is no authority except that which God has established. The authorities that exist have been established by God." (Romans 13:1)

For many years as the final judge and one of the first prophets, Samuel led the nation of Israel. But he grew old, so he appointed his sons as leaders. In 1 Samuel 8:3, Scripture tells us Samuel's sons were dishonest, took bribes, perverted justice, and did not follow God's ways. The elders in Israel came to Samuel and asked for a king so they could be like the other nations around them. Samuel was devastated at this request.

God spoke to Samuel saying the Jewish people had not rejected him, but God Himself. Ever since God brought the people of Israel out of Egypt, they had often followed other gods. And now they wanted a physical leader that they could see rather than follow the one true God. "'Now listen to them; but warn them solemnly and let them know what the king who will reign over them will claim as his rights'" (1 Samuel 8:9).

The aging prophet warned the people that a king would take their sons and daughters and part of their land. The people listened to this warning but continued to ask Samuel for a king. "The LORD answered, 'Listen to them and give them a king'" (1 Samuel 8:22). The Book of Samuel then details how a Benjaminite named Kish had a handsome son, Saul (who stood a head taller than everyone else). One day Kish lost some donkeys and asked Saul to go with a servant and look for them. The pair searched many different places without success. The servant suggested they visit a seer named Samuel who lived nearby. Little did they know that Samuel was waiting for them. God had revealed to the prophet the day before, "'About this time tomorrow I will send you a man from the land of Benjamin. Anoint him ruler over my people Israel; he will deliver them from the hand of the Philistines. I have looked on my people, for their cry has reached me'" (1 Samuel 9:16).

The prophet reassured Saul that the donkeys had been found and encouraged him to stay with him overnight. Early the next morning Samuel took Saul to the roof of his home and anointed him with oil. This simple farmer was transformed into a king. At age 30, Saul became the first king of Israel and ruled for 42 years (1 Samuel 13:1). While he didn't expect it—perhaps didn't want it—Saul became the leader of Israel.

Within the church, businesses, and even families, there are always sudden shifts in leadership. Many of these changes are unexpected and unplanned. Have you been involved in one of these changes in your life? What changes did you make to rise to the occasion? Or what mistakes did you make which were detrimental to that relationship? Relationships are fluid and can change at any moment. Be committed to responding well in order to keep the relationship more important than how the effect of the change.

Pivot from feeling that change in your sphere of influence is always a bad thing.

Pivot to a belief that God can work in every change, no matter how painful, and is able to grow your own faith through that change.

Prayer
"Throughout my days, Lord, change is something I can depend on to happen—in my work, in my church, and in my family. When it happens, help me to turn to You for guidance and strength to make the right choice that brings peace and order. In Jesus' name."

Your Pivotal Moment of Faith
Reflect on a time of sudden change or transition in your own life where you became the leader or suddenly had to leave a company or church or family. Did you grow spiritually from the experience? What lessons can you learn for your next transition or change?

Josiah: Discovery of the Law and Change

"When your words came, I ate them; they were my joy and my heart's delight, for I bear your name, LORD God Almighty." (Jeremiah 15:16)

The nation of Israel was split into a northern kingdom, Israel, and a southern kingdom, Judah. Some of the Judean kings were known as good because they followed the ways of God, but others were bad because they guided their people away from God. Under the rule of King Manasseh the people turned to evil and followed other gods. The temple in Jerusalem fell into ruin and lack of use. And even though he had a dramatic change of heart near the end of his life, the damage had been done. At the end of King Manasseh's life, his son, Amon, took over and followed his father's pattern of evil. Amon ruled for only two years until one of his officials assassinated him. In the middle of this chaos, the priest installed Amon's eight-year-old son, Josiah as the replacement monarch.

Unlike his grandfather and father, King Josiah was a godly man. And eight years later at the age of 16, he began to seek the Lord (2 Chronicles 34:3). Josiah was dedicated to instituting and restarting the worship of God. When Josiah was 20, he ordered the pagan centers of worship in the land to be torn down (2 Chronicles 34:4). This removal process was extensive, and the changes took several years of work.

Finally, when he was 26 years old, King Josiah turned and ordered the repair of the Lord's temple in Jerusalem (2 Chronicles 34:8). The damage to God's house was extensive and during the cleanup, Hilkiah, the priest, found the Book of the Law and brought the scroll to King Josiah. They read the scroll, and the experience distressed the king's soul. As he heard the words of God's law for the first time, and began to glimpse the anger God must have towards this sinful people, Josiah ripped his clothing and wept (2 Chronicles 34:19,27).

As described in the Law, King Josiah ordered the reinstitution of the regular sacrifices and the annual celebrations of the feasts, including the Passover. Throughout his life, King Josiah listened to instructions from the Lord, and it changed his kingdom and his people for the good. It's interesting to note that the prophet Jeremiah wrote the Bible account of this story found in 2 Kings 22–23. The priest who found the book of the Law, Hilkiah, was Jeremiah's father.

While our world is much different from the ancient world of Judah, evil—and good—exist in abundance. If you watch the evening news, you've noticed that people are consistently committing violent acts of evil against others. But, also in our world, there are nonprofit groups like the Salvation Army or local churches who open their doors to the homeless and help the poor. In a world of good and evil, do all you can to put some points on the board in the "good" category.

Pivot from becoming apathetic to evil and lazy toward the good.

Pivot to a proactive approach of helping others so that they can move through life and their faith journey in ways that show God cares for their every need.

Prayer
"Thank you, Lord, for how You have preserved the Scriptures through the ages so we can have them and read Your Word. Help us to get more of Your words into our everyday life. Amen."

Your Pivotal Moment of Faith
According to some, there are roughly 900 English translations of the Bible. Take a moment and imagine the excitement when Hilkiah and King Josiah found the only book of the Law of God after it had been lost for years. Make a recommitment to do more reading of the Bible in your everyday life.

Hezekiah: Gravely Ill to Reformer

"Praise the LORD, my soul, and forget not all his benefits—who forgives all your sins and heals all your diseases." (Psalm 103:2-3)

Among the kings of Judah, Hezekiah was the son of King Ahaz . . . who was an evil king. There is an unusual sentence about Hezekiah: "Hezekiah trusted in the LORD, the God of Israel. There was no one like him among all the kings of Judah, either before him or after him" (2 Kings 18:5). Known as a reformer who faithfully followed the Lord. The King fell ill, and the Lord sent the prophet Isaiah to speak with the king to get his affairs in order because he was going to die.

When he heard this news from the prophet, King Hezekiah, wept bitterly and prayed, "'Remember, LORD, how I have walked before you faithfully and with wholehearted devotion and have done what is good in your eyes'" (2 Kings 20:3). The Lord heard the king's prayer and before Isaiah could leave the middle court of the palace, God commanded the prophet to return to the king.

"'Go back and tell Hezekiah, the ruler of my people, "This is what the LORD, the God of your father David, says: I have heard your prayer and seen your tears; I will heal you. On the third day from now you will go up to the temple of the LORD. I will add fifteen years to your life. And I will deliver you and this city from the hand of the king of

Assyria. I will defend this city for my sake and for the sake of my servant David'" (2 Kings 20:5-6). The prophet then prepared a medicated paste of figs for the King's boil, and it healed him.

King Hezekiah had questions for Isaiah. "How will I know that the Lord has healed me?"

Looking to a nearby stairway, the prophet answered, "The shadow on the stairs could go forward 10 steps or backward 10 steps."

"It normally goes forward so it would be a miracle for it to go backward," Hezekiah explained. Isaiah prayed, and the shadow moved backwards 10 steps. God performed a miracle of healing, and it added 15 years to the life of the king.

Throughout the Bible and including this story about King Hezekiah, we learn that God cares about our health. The Scriptures encourage us to pray and ask for God's guidance and healing. Sometimes the Lord uses medicine and doctors. Other times God heals. For our prayers, there are three answers: "yes," "no," and "not yet." The third option is one of the most difficult for every believer. As Christians, we trust God to guide the timing and the details of our everyday lives—including our health and our healing.

Pivot from believing that God can't, won't or is indifferent toward helping you along the path that you should go.

Pivot to a firm knowledge that while I plan my way, it's the Lord who directs my steps.

Prayer

"Father, thank You for this story of how You guided and healed King Hezekiah. Increase my faith to trust in You for my daily health as You answer my prayers. In Jesus' name, amen."

Your Pivotal Moment of Faith

Consider some periods in your life where God has answered prayers. Then also recall the times where the answer has been "not yet." What actions can you take to celebrate that our lives are a faith journey and not one to be lived by sight alone?

Gideon: From Fear and Insecurity to Confidence

"When I am afraid, I put my trust in you."
(Psalm 56:3, ESV)

For forty years the Jewish people lived in peace. Yet during this period the people turned away from God and to evil (Judges 6:1). As punishment for their disobedience, God had their neighbors, the Midianites, attack and oppress them for seven years. When the Israelites planted their crops, the Midianites would swoop into the land and take the food and livestock. In near starvation, the Israelites cried out to the Lord for His help.

The Lord answers the prayers of His people. One day an angel of the Lord sat under an oak tree in Ophrah which belonged to Joash the Abiezrite. The angel watched Joash's son, Gideon, thresh wheat in a winepress to hide it from the Midianites. The angel said to Gideon, "The Lord is with you, mighty warrior."

Gideon shook his head at these words saying, "I don't understand, if the Lord is with us why are the Midianites attacking us and where are the miracles and wonders our ancestors tell us that the Lord does for His people? It looks like the Lord has abandoned us and given us to the Midianites."

The angel said, "You have the strength to save Israel from the Midianites. I'm sending you."

Gideon held out his hand in objection, "How in the world could I save Israel? I'm from the weakest clan in the tribe of Manasseh, and I am the least in my family."

The angel said, "I will be with you, and you will kill all of the Midianites and none will escape alive."

"If it pleases you, please don't go away until I go home and bring a sacrificial offering to you," Gideon said.

"Okay, I will wait until you return."

Gideon prepared a young goat and some unleavened bread. When he returned the angel touched the meat and the bread with the staff in his hand and it was consumed with fire. In the same way he appeared, the angel disappeared.

Later, still unsure if God wanted him to lead the Israelites, Gideon prayed and proposed a test, "'If you will save Israel by my hand as you have promised—look, I will place a wool fleece on the threshing floor. If there is dew only on the fleece and all the ground is dry, then I will know that you will save Israel by my hand, as you said.' And that is what happened. Gideon rose early the next day; he squeezed the fleece and wrung out the dew—a bowlful of water" (Judges 6:36-38). Then Gideon asked to have the miracle repeated, but reversed, with the ground wet and the fleece dry. Once again, the Lord confirmed His promise.

Confident of his leadership, Gideon gathered the people and with 300 men and trumpets, he stationed them around the Midianite army. Frightened, the Midianites turned on each other and Gideon succeeded in rescuing the nation of Israel.

At first, Gideon was afraid but as he prayed and God affirmed his actions with the fleece, his fear changed to faith. Do you have something in your life that is making you afraid? Maybe it's a challenge at work or in your family or in your church. Use the experience of Gideon to change your fear into a mighty faith.

Pivot from the possible fear you have that God might call you to be his instrument for good in the lives of others.

Pivot to becoming more expectant that God could use you to impact someone else's life.

Prayer
"God, in times of fear, give me the faith to put my trust in You. In Jesus' name."

Your Pivotal Moment of Faith
Think about a time in your life when you were afraid. How can you use the story of Gideon to change your fear into faith in God?

Shadrach, Meshach and Abednego: Refusal to Compromise

"Love the LORD your God with all your heart and with all your soul and with all your strength."
(Deuteronomy 6:5)

When the Babylonian army conquered Israel, the victors took a number of the handsome and attractive young men to Babylon. These captives were taught the language and local customs. While they served in this foreign land, King Nebuchadnezzar had a ninety-foot tall and nine-foot-wide image of himself built and set it up on the plain of Dura in the province of Babylon.

Soon after, the king called an assembly with the various leaders, governors, and judges. The herald loudly proclaimed in every language, "Whenever you hear a horn, bagpipe, or any other type of music, each of you are to fall face down and worship this image of King Nebuchadnezzar. If you don't immediately fall down, then you will be thrown into a furnace of blazing fire."

This group of leaders noticed that three Jewish men who the King appointed to lead Babylon paid no attention to the music or this new law. Their names were Shadrach, Meshach and Abednego. The group of leaders called out this violation to the king saying, "These Jewish men ignore your new law." The King ordered these men to be brought before him.

When the three men arrived before the statue, the king ordered the music to sound and everyone except Shadrach, Meshach and Abednego fell down in worship. The king was furious at the violation of his new law. "Who can rescue you from the fiery furnace?"

The men answered, "The God we serve is able to deliver us from it, and he will deliver us from Your Majesty's hand. But even if he does not, we want you to know, Your Majesty, that we will not serve your gods or worship the image of gold you have set up" (Daniel 3:17-18).

That answer made the king's anger increase, "Heat up the furnace for these three men." The King ordered it to be seven times hotter than normal. Shadrach, Meshach and Abednego were bound and thrown into the fire. It was so hot; it even killed the men who threw them into the fire!

As the king watched, he could see four men walking around in the fire—instead of the expected trio. He called to them, "Shadrach, Meshach and Abednego, come out of the furnace." When they climbed out of the furnace nothing was damaged or even smelled of smoke. Amazed, he immediately said, "I declare no one can speak out against the God of Shadrach, Meshach and Abednego."

This story shows us the importance of following God's commands in spite of the consequences. Living with integrity and following the promises in Scripture is more important than some conflict with a manmade rule or regulation. As believers, we need to trust God to rescue us from any compromise or rule-breaking situation. If He doesn't rescue us, we will know for certain we have been loyal to the Scriptures in word and deed.

Pivot from a fear of what men could do to you if you choose to follow closely with God.

Pivot to the conviction that courageous faith may have consequences but so does ignoring the privilege of standing firm for what you know to be true.

Prayer
"Father God, thank You that You are the Lord of the universe. As I follow Your words, guide my steps and help me to remember You are in charge of my every action. In Jesus' name."

Your Pivotal Moment of Faith
Think about a time when you were pressured to compromise a standard or break a rule. How did you handle it? What promise can you make to the Lord for how you will handle it in the future?

Miriam: A Lesson in Humility

"Guide me in your truth and teach me, for you are God my Savior, and my hope is in you all day long." (Psalm 25:5)

Centuries had passed since Joseph was second in command in Egypt. The current Pharoah knew nothing about Joseph. In fact, this leader enslaved the Hebrews and ordered the midwives to kill any male babies to keep the Hebrew population in check. The midwives refused.

Still, when one Hebrew mother gave birth to a son, she hid him. And when he was too old to hide, she put her baby into a reed basket on the Nile River and asked her older daughter, Miriam, to watch what happened to the baby. As Miriam watched from a hidden place, one of Pharoah's daughters found the baby. Thinking quickly, Miriam asked Pharoah's daughter if she needed a nurse for the baby. "Great idea" the daughter said. So Miriam ran to her own mother who then became a nurse for own son, who was now called Moses.

Raised as a member of Pharoah's household as a young man, Moses eventually fled to the desert after killing an Egyptian. His new job was to care for sheep in Midian. Many decades later, God called him back to Egypt to release the Hebrew people. His older sister, Miriam, practically disappears from the Bible stories until much later when they were traveling in the desert. For many years the Lord designated Moses as the leader of the Hebrews and even entrusted him with delivering the ten commandments to the Jewish nation.

We see Miriam enter the story again while the Israelites camped at Hazeroth. Miriam, and her brother Aaron stirred up the people to complain about Moses because he was married to a foreign woman. They complained, "Has the Lord only spoken through Moses? Hasn't He spoken through us too?"

Immediately the Lord called Moses, Aaron, and Miriam to stand before the tent of meeting. "He said, listen to my words: 'When there is a prophet among you, I, the LORD, reveal myself to them in visions, I speak to them in dreams. But this is not true of my servant Moses; he is faithful in all my house. With him I speak face to face, clearly and not in riddles; he sees the form of the LORD. Why then were you not afraid to speak against my servant Moses?' The anger of the LORD burned against them, and he left them" (Numbers 12:6-9).

When the cloud of the Lord rose, Miriam had become a leper. Seeing the punishment for his sister, Moses cried out to the Lord for her healing. The Lord instructed that Miriam be confined outside of the camp for seven days. The entire camp waited for seven days until Miriam was healed from the leprosy. While the Bible doesn't tell us anything else about this incident, it likely humbled Miriam and gave her a different perspective on the leadership of her brother Moses.

While it is unlikely God would make you a leper to teach you humility, it's an essential lesson in life. In your work or at home, many conflicts arise to help you understand humility. How have these character-building incidents helped you and guided your interactions with others?

Pivot from the "world revolves around me and my needs" attitude.

Pivot to the conviction that every conflict can bring an opportunity to understand the virtue of humility as you listen to the voice of others speaking into your life.

Prayer
"God, as I do my part to lead my family, my work, my church and neighborhood, help me to have the right attitude of humility and lean on You to guide my thoughts and steps. I need You . . . every hour. Amen."

Your Pivotal Moment of Faith
It's a common expression: "too big for their britches." Have you ever expressed such an attitude in the family or at work or at church? Recall the story and let it guide you to have more balance in your life.

Joshua: Stepping Up to Lead

"Keep this Book of the Law always on your lips; meditate on it day and night, so that you may be careful to do everything written in it. Then you will be prosperous and successful." (Joshua 1:8)

One of the greatest leaders in the Old Testament was Moses. He seemed like he was in constant communication with God, especially through the ten plagues God used to deal with the Egyptian leaders. Moses led the people out of bondage and through the Red Sea.

Joshua, son of Nun, was Moses' assistant. Exodus 17:9 marks the first mention of Joshua in the Bible as he led the Israelites into battle with the Amalekites. When Moses climbed Mount Siani to receive the ten commandments, Joshua went with him and helped him with the Tent of Meeting. Beyond his work as Moses' assistant, Joshua was one of the twelve spies sent from Kadesh into the land of Canaan to explore it. With Caleb, Joshua was one of two people who gave a good report about the promised land of Canaan. But because the people didn't have courage and faith to follow the Lord into Canaan, the Lord sentenced them to remain in the wilderness another forty years. Caleb and Joshua were the only two older adults who entered Canaan.

While the Scriptures do not give many details, Joshua must have learned a great deal as the assistant to Moses. Ultimately, because of a grievous sin Moses committed, he was not allowed to lead the Jewish people into the Promised Land. Instead, Moses climbed a mountain and saw Canaan in the distance. He remained on the mountain until his death. Joshua stepped into the leadership role and brought the people to conquer the Promised Land.

God gave Joshua special instructions about how to cross the overflowing Jordan River—the boundary into Canaan. It was too deep to cross easily, but when the priest's feet who carried the Ark of the Covenant touched the water, the water upstream stopped! The people walked across on dry ground—then the priests came across and immediately the river returned to normal. Joshua's leadership throughout this miraculous event was evident.

Soon after, at God's specific direction, Joshua led the people to march around the city walls of Jericho for seven days. The final day, God destroyed the Jericho walls, and they captured the city.

Pivot from leaning on your own power and understanding.

Pivot to a deeper appreciation of how God works and a greater knowledge of the Kingdom principles throughout the Bible.

Prayer

"Lord, whether I am an assistant or a leader, guide my steps and teach me the lessons of faithful obedience from Scripture. Thank You for this example from Joshua and how he learned from the example and life of Moses. Amen."

Your Pivotal Moment of Faith

Think about the various pastors or leaders in your business when there was a change in leadership. What lessons from the life of Joshua can you add to your life? Read the story of Joshua's commission to leadership and memorize the verse in today's reading. As you meditate on this Scripture, write some ideas about how you can keep God's Word on your heart and lips.

Elisha: Leaving Family to Follow God's Leading

"A person's steps are directed by the LORD. How then can anyone understand their own way?"
(Proverbs 20:24)

The prophet Elijah had fled to the desert to escape the wrath of Queen Jezebel who threatened to kill him. He boldly asked to see God, and so the Lord asked the prophet to stand on a mountain. A fierce windstorm blew, then a loud earthquake shook the ground, and then a massive fire blazed. The Lord was not in the wind, the earthquake, or the fire.

Finally, Elijah heard a gentle whisper. His response was to cover his face. He knew he was hearing God's voice. The Lord asked, "What are you doing here, Elijah?" (1 Kings 19:13). Then God gave him a series of specific instructions including "'... anoint Elisha son of Shaphat from Abel Meholah to succeed you as prophet" (1 Kings 19:16b).

The prophet found Elisha in the field plowing with his oxen. The older prophet threw his cloak around Elisha who then asked permission to say goodbye to his parents. Oxen were sacrificed, and the younger Elisha followed Elijah and served the old prophet throughout his final days on earth.

Months later, both of them knew that Elijah was about to be taken directly to God. Other prophets also knew the old prophet was going to leave and gave this information to Elisha. Several times Elijah asked his assistant to leave him, but Elisha refused. After several exchanges and travels to different places, the old prophet asked Elisha if there was anything he wanted before he was taken. In a bold request, Elisha answered, "Let me inherit a double portion of your spirit."

"You have asked a difficult thing," Elijah said, "yet if you see me when I am taken from you, it will be yours—otherwise, it will not" (2 Kings 2:9-10). Moments later, as Elisha watched, chariots of fire and horses came down from the sky to the earth. And the old prophet Elijah disappeared in a whirlwind. After his master left, Elisha picked up the old prophet's cloak. When Elisha struck the water, it divided to the right and left. He walked across on dry ground. Because he inherited a double portion of Elijah's spirit, throughout the rest of his ministry Elisha performed a number of miracles.

These days, God doesn't always have to give us such specific directions like he did for Elijah and Elisha. Instead, we have the Scriptures and can read them day in and day out. These words will guide our daily actions, if we turn our heart toward hearing and following instructions as the Lord gives them to us.

Pivot from following the shouts and bluster that the world tries to make you follow so as to distract you from a sincere faith.

Pivot to following the still small voice of God by choosing to allow His Spirit the chance to speak to you each day.

Prayer

"Heavenly Father, thank You for the Bible and how You use it to speak to in gentle ways. Use these words and stories to direct my daily steps. Help me to meditate on You and gain your daily wisdom. Amen."

Your Pivotal Moment of Faith

Do you feel like you're hearing God speak to you on a regular basis? If not, is it because you've allowed the noise and clutter around you to drown out the voice of God? For the next few weeks, try to find a place of quiet to hear from God in prayer and through the Scriptures.

Jethro: Wise Counselor

"If any of you lacks wisdom, you should ask God, who gives generously to all without finding fault, and it will be given to you." (James 1:5)

When Moses fled Egypt, he went to the desert of Midian. Some women were waiting to water their sheep. Moses helped them get their water and these women returned home early. Jethro, their father, asked them, "Why did you get home early?" When he heard about the Egyptian who had helped his daughters, he invited Moses to spend time with his family. That incident was the start of Moses' relationship with Jethro. After a few years, Moses married one of Jethro's daughters and cared for his flocks. Later, through the burning bush, the Lord called Moses back to Egypt and caused a series of ten plagues which ended in the release of the Jewish people into the wilderness. As the people were in the wilderness, Jethro re-entered the biblical story when he brought his daughter and children to Moses.

As Jethro stayed with Moses for a few days, he observed his son-in-law. For every decision, large or small, the people brought it directly to Moses. Throughout the day from early morning until late at night, the people came to Moses for wise judgments.

Moses' father-in-law replied, "What you are doing is not good. You and these people who come to you will only wear yourselves out. The work is too heavy for you; you cannot handle it alone. Listen now to me and I will give you some advice, and may God be with you. You must be the people's representative before God and bring their disputes to him. Teach them his decrees and instructions and show them the way they are to live and how they are to behave. But select capable men from all the people—men who fear God, trustworthy men who hate dishonest gain—and appoint them as officials over thousands, hundreds, fifties and tens. Have them serve as judges for the people at all times but have them bring every difficult case to you; the simple cases they can decide themselves. That will make your load lighter, because they will share it with you. If you do this and God so commands, you will be able to stand the strain, and all these people will go home satisfied" (Exodus 18:17-23).

Moses listened to his father-in-law and followed his advice which was a turning point in how he led the Jewish people. Other leaders made the simple decisions, and only the difficult rulings were brought to Moses.

Where do you get advice, counsel, and wisdom? Maybe it is a mentor in your work or an older person in your church who you meet with on a regular basis. Or possibly it is a counselor who helps you in difficult situations. Even a leader like Moses needed someone like Jethro to give him wise advice.

Pivot from thinking you've got the market cornered on wisdom, especially as it relates to how you spend the hours you have each week to help others.

Pivot to seeking out people who know you well enough to speak into how you can most effectively serve other people.

Prayer

"Father, help me to speak to the right friends and leaders as I seek wisdom from them when I accept the challenge of helping others. Thank You for using these people in my life. In Jesus' name. Amen."

Your Pivotal Moment of Faith

Do you have a current life challenge that you are trying to handle on your own? What can you learn from the life of Moses and Jethro that you can carry into your own life?

Caleb: Unwavering Faith

"Let us hold unswervingly to the hope we profess, for he who promised is faithful." (Hebrews 10:23)

Through a series of plagues on the Egyptians the Lord brought the Jewish people out of slavery in order to fulfill His promise to move them into the Promised Land. Throughout that experience of walking though the Red Sea, being fed manna, not being ill or having their shoes or clothing wear out—and many other miracles of survival—some people took those marvels for granted. But not Caleb.

This son of Jephunneh from the tribe of Judah stood out from the others on the journey. When they reached the edge of Canaan, Moses selected twelve men to check out the land and report back to the people. Caleb was one of those dozen men. Numbers says, "The LORD said to Moses, 'Send men to explore Canaan, which I'm giving to the Israelites. From each ancestral tribe send one of its leaders" (Numbers 13:1-2).

Before those leaders left, Moses gave them a series of instructions for their tasks in the land saying, "Go up through the Negev and on into the hill country. See what the land is like and whether the people who live there are strong or weak, few or many. What kind of land do they live in? Is it good or bad? What kind of towns do they live in?

Are they unwalled or fortified? How is the soil? Is it fertile or poor? Are there trees in it or not?" (Numbers 13:17-20).

More than a report, Moses asked them to bring samples of the local produce and grapes which were in season and beginning to ripen. The men went into the land, and ten of the spies came back with a report the land was rich with milk and honey yet also had giant-sized people in the land and recommended staying away. Two of them, Joshua, Moses' assistant in war, and Caleb had the opposite report. "Then Caleb silenced the people before Moses and said, 'We should go up and take possession of the land, for we can certainly do it.'" (Numbers 13:30).

The fearful report overpowered the faithful report of Caleb. As punishment God sent the people back into the desert for forty years until all of those unfaithful people had died. Two of these leaders remained alive and saw the promised land: Joshua and Caleb. After the conquest of Canaan, Caleb said, "Now then, just as the LORD promised, he has kept me alive for forty-five years since the time he said this to Moses, while Israel moved about in the wilderness. So here I am today, eighty-five years old! I am still as strong today as the day Moses sent me out; I'm just as vigorous to go out to battle now as I was then." (Joshua 14:10-11). Joshua blessed Caleb and gave him Hebron as his inheritance.

The life of Caleb gives us an example of someone who practiced a life of optimistic faith. For us, when giant trials come into our lives, it's easy to be consumed with fear instead of firmly grounded belief. Through the story of Caleb, we can celebrate someone who continues to trust God in the face of uncertainty and fear. Everyone has challenges such as a sick child, a broken appliance, or a car that needs repair. With each of these situations, learn to grow your faith and trust in our Heavenly Father instead of wallowing in fear of the moment.

Pivot from believing that God isn't interested in the small details of our life.

Pivot to knowing that God loves, God listens, and God answers even the smallest cares that weigh on our heart.

Prayer
"Lord when trials come help me to increase my faith in You. In Your strong name, amen."

Your Pivotal Moment of Faith
How can you use the story of Caleb to strengthen your faith and trust in our Heavenly Father?

Hagar: Resilience and Faith in the Face of Hardship

"Endure hardship as discipline; God is treating you as his children. For what children are not disciplined by their father?" (Hebrews 12:7)

When does your patience run out? God promised Abram that He would become a nation as numerous as the stars in the sky. For ten years, Abram had faithfully waited for the Lord to fulfill this promise. When both of them, Abram and his wife, Sarai, were well past the age of childbearing, Sarai took matters into her own hands. She gave her Egyptian maid Hagar to sleep with her husband and produce a child.

When Hagar became pregnant with Abram's child, Sarai suddenly despised her maid (Genesis 16:4). Abram told Sarai to do whatever she wanted with Hagar. Sarai treated her maid with harshness and caused pregnant Hagar to flee into the desert to escape. When she reached a well, the angel of the Lord came to Hagar and asked, "Where have you come from and where are you going?"

With a straight-forward answer, Hagar said, "I'm running away from the presence of my mistress Sarai."

With a shake of his head, the angel of the Lord told Hagar, "Return to your mistress and submit yourself to her hand. In fact, you will have many descendants." Then the angel gave Hagar this promise.

"You are now pregnant, and you will give birth to a son. You shall name him Ishmael, for the LORD has heard of your misery. He will be a wild donkey of a man; his hand will be against everyone, and everyone's hand against him, and he will live in hostility toward all his brothers" (Genesis 16:11-12).

As hard as it must have been, Hagar obeyed the angel, returned to Sarai, and bore a son whom she named Ishmael. While Hagar's faith and obedience seem like a side-story to the main story of faith from Abraham and Sarah, our own faith and obedience is often a side story to much of who God brings into our lives. Yet keeping the faith is an essential element to the hundreds of others we might touch in our lifetime.

Pivot from the belief that your own story of faith might not have any impact with those in your sphere of influence.

Pivot to a quiet and patient faith that understands that trust and obedience have a small but essential role in the faith of others.

Prayer
"Lord, help me to patiently follow your guidance even when things get hard and difficult. I trust in You. In Jesus' name. Amen"

Your Pivotal Moment of Faith

Renew your efforts to faithfully follow the Lord through seasons of hardship. Think about a time when you took matters into your own hands for a decision instead of patiently being obedient to the LORD's direction. How could you have changed your decisions to allow God time and ways to grow the faith of another through you?

Jonah: The Reluctant Evangelist

"In all your ways submit to him, and he will make your paths straight." (Proverbs 3:6)

Have you ever run in the opposite direction from a clear command from God? Like maybe loving someone in your life who was difficult to love. My guess is you didn't have to taste and smell the inside of a big fish to get you back on track. But that is exactly what happened to Jonah after the Lord commanded him to preach to the wicked city of Nineveh. Because God can always see the 30,000-foot view of life, He knew Jonah's message would move those people to repent. Like a small child, instead of following God's command to go to Nineveh, Jonah boarded a ship in Joppa going the opposite direction to Tarsus.

Because the Lord was not happy with Jonah's choice, He sent strong winds and waves to the ship. The sailors on the ship were doing everything possible to save their vessel from imminent catastrophe. If they could discard anything off the ship to help themselves, they tossed it overboard to keep their vessel from sinking. Also, each of them was praying to their different gods for help with the storm . . . but nothing seemed to work.

Then they found Jonah who was sound asleep in the hold of the ship. When they woke him, Jonah explained he was fleeing from God. "This storm is my fault because I am running away from God.

Just throw me overboard and the storm will stop." Reluctant to take such drastic action with their passenger, the men tried to row the boat to shore but the storm grew stronger. Finally, they agreed to throw Jonah overboard because they had tried everything else. And sure enough, when Jonah went into the sea, the storm stopped.

A giant fish swallowed Jonah, and he spent three days in the belly of this fish before he repented and told God, "If you save my life, I will go to Nineveh." The fish spit Jonah out on dry land and he soon traveled to the wicked city. As he preached for the people to change from their evil ways, the people listened and responded. The king of Nineveh tore his clothes and put on sack cloth and ashes. Other people followed the king's example. The people turned to God and the Lord spared the destruction of the city.

Are you ignoring God's nudge to reach out to those whom He's asked you to speak to? If so, you're missing a double blessing. The first is the joy of helping another understand the Kingdom of God. The second is the joy of obeying the Spirit's calling to use you in someone else's life.

Pivot from a numb heart toward loving people whom God loves.

Pivot to the realization that *you* may be the person God wants to send to another to show them His love, or to move them out of the doldrums of life into something vibrant.

Prayer

"Heavenly Father, thank You for the difficult people in my life—souls whom You love. Give me the courage to speak truth and love to them when the time is right so they can understand the depth of Your grace."

Your Pivotal Moment of Faith

Think about the difficult people in your life. Write down a name or two, and when you do, pray that God would use you in some way to move them forward toward a genuine love and faith in Him.

Solomon: Learning the Key Duty of Man

"Now all has been heard; here is the conclusion of the matter: Fear God and keep his commandments, for this is the duty of all mankind."
(Ecclesiastes 12:13)

An unsettled feeling was brewing in the royal family of King David in Israel. Since they had an aging monarch, the people knew that they were watching the final days of his reign. Years earlier, King David promised Solomon's mother Bathsheba that her son would be the next ruler (1 Kings 1:11-13), but many had forgotten that promise. King David had many sons and Adonijah, who was older than Solomon, set himself up to be the next king and threw a coronation party with several leaders including Abiathar the priest. When Bathsheba and the prophet Nathan heard about this coronation, they went to David and asked about it. At David's request and before his death, Solomon was anointed the new King of Israel.

Early in his reign, King Solomon went to Gibeon and offered a thousand sacrifices on the altar. In a dream, the Lord appeared to Solomon and said, "Ask from me whatever you want." The young king could have asked for anything such as great wealth or a long life. Instead, Solomon responded saying,

"God, you were kind to my father, David, and now please show your kindness to me. Give me your wisdom to lead your people and to know the difference between right and wrong."

This prayer pleased the Lord. "God said to him, 'Since you have asked for this and not for long life or wealth for yourself, nor have asked for the death of your enemies but for discernment in administering justice, I will do what you have asked. I will give you a wise and discerning heart, so that there will never be anyone like you, nor will there ever be. Moreover, I will give you what you have not asked for—both wealth and honor—so that in your lifetime you will have no equal among kings. And if you walk in obedience to me and keep my decrees and commands as David your father did, I will give you a long life" (1 Kings 3: 11-14).

Throughout history, no one was wiser than Solomon. People came from across the world to marvel at his wisdom and words, plus God gave him riches and a long life. In spite of his wisdom, Solomon had 700 wives and 300 concubines. Some of these women drew Solomon away from the Lord to their gods. However, the book of Ecclesiastes suggests that Solomon eventually recognized the futility of life without God, pivoting back to the realization that fearing God and keeping His commandments is the whole duty of man.

Even someone as wise as Solomon can be drawn away from a relationship with God. Your idol might not be another god but maybe it is your work, your family, your friends, hobbies, or some other distraction to blur your focus on Christ. And if we're not connected to God, we will likely be dull in our desire to help others.

Pivot from the distractions of life that cause you to turn away from your first love.

Pivot to more of an undivided heart and a focused life that moves you to follow the Great Commandment: Love the Lord your God with all of your heart, soul and strength . . . and to love your neighbor as yourself.

Prayer
"Lord God, guide my life so I remember the Creator and Sustainer of all my days. Forgive me when I have been pulled away with something else and guide my steps to return to Your and Your Word. Amen."

Your Pivotal Moment of Faith
With a journal or a legal pad, take a few moments and reflect on the overall purpose of your life. How much of your thought life is focused on God. How can you pivot and increase your time in prayer and reading God's Word?

Mary Magdalene: A Life-changing Encounter with Jesus

"Praise the LORD, my soul, and forget not all his benefits—who forgives all your sins and heals all your diseases." (Psalm 103:2-3)

Throughout the three-year earthly ministry of Jesus Christ, He would often heal people of demon possession. These demons were never kind to the person they possessed (see Mark 9:14-29), so Jesus commanded the demons, "Come out of this person."

These stories about Jesus show the Savior's great compassion. And some of those who were healed, chose to follow Jesus afterwards. Besides the twelve disciples who always traveled with Jesus, Luke 8:2-3 says that among those following Jesus were, "some women who had been cured of evil spirits and diseases: Mary (called Magdalene) from whom seven demons had come out; Joanna the wife of Chuza, the manager of Herod's household; Susanna; and many others. These women were helping to support them out of their own means."

When Jesus cast out seven demons from Mary, the experience naturally changed her life. In gratitude, Mary joined a small group of women who helped support the life-changing message of Jesus.

During the final days of His ministry, Jesus came to Jerusalem, had a final meal with His disciples and spent time in prayer in the Garden of Gethsemane. The Messiah knew He would be crucified for the sins of the world. As He carried His cross to Golgotha—and was then forcibly nailed to it—the Gospel of Mark tells us who was watching these events: "Some women were watching from a distance. Among them were Mary Magdalene, Mary the mother of James, the younger son of Joseph, and Salome. In Galilee these women had followed him and cared for his needs. Many other women who had come up with him to Jerusalem were also there" (Mark 15:40-41).

Mary and the other women watched Jesus die and then heard that Joseph of Arimathea asked Pilate to take His body to a cave hewn out of stone—a place of burial that Joseph gave up in honor of Jesus. They saw where the soldiers left the body of Jesus, and how a giant stone was rolled over the entrance to close the grave. A few days later, Mary Magdalene was among the women who went to anoint the body of Jesus; preparing it more thoroughly for burial, as was their custom. When they walked toward the grave, they wondered how they would be able to move the gravestone. To their surprise, the tomb was open—and empty! Mark 16:9 says Mary Magdelene was the first to see the risen Savior. Though when she told His disciples they did not believe her story.

Many of Mary's actions in the New Testament sprang from her gratitude that Jesus healed her demonic possession. How much gratitude do you have in your daily life? Thanking people in words and deeds needs to be a key part of our response as a devoted follower of Jesus. Gratitude to God is essential, but gratitude to those who have helped us along the way is also a great response when our life has been altered for the good by another fellow traveler.

Pivot from being so proud and self-focused that you forget those who have helped you along your path.

Pivot to having an "attitude of gratitude" to God—and others who have enriched your life.

Prayer
"Father, help me to have a heart of gratitude and to follow the example of Mary Magdalene. Thank You for all You have done in my life and continue to do day in and day out. And thank You for those You've sent to my life to show me the vastness of God's love. Amen."

Your Pivotal Moment of Faith
Purchase a package of thank you notes and commit to handwriting one or two thank you notes every week. It is rare for anyone to send such a note, and your gratitude will be appreciated.

Samson: His Final Prayer

"The LORD is my strength and my shield; my heart trusts in him, and he helps me. My heart leaps for joy, and with my song I praise him." (Psalm 28:7)

Throughout the period of the judges in the Bible, the Israelites often did evil in the eyes of the Lord and He delivered them into the hands of the Philistines, or other nations. Soon, Israel would cry out for deliverance and God would send a judge to deliver them. Peace would prevail for a few decades until the cycle repeated itself. Samson's story begins while, under the weight of persecution from the Philistines, the Israelites called out to the Lord.

A man named Manoah from the tribe of Dan had a wife who was childless. One night an angel of the Lord appeared to Manoah's wife, the only time she is mentioned in Scripture, and declared she would have a child. He was never to cut his hair, and from the womb he would be a Nazarite—someone dedicated to God. He would deliver Israel from the Philistines. This wife told her husband about the angel and Manoah asked to see the angel, who reappeared and told him the same details.

As promised, a son was born, and they named him Samson. He kept his lifetime vow to not cut his hair and the Lord gave Samson great strength. Samson often clashed with the Philistines. On one occasion, he burned their grain fields along with their vineyards and olive groves (Judges 15:3-5).

On another occasion, using the jawbone of a donkey, Samson killed a thousand Philistines (Judges 15:15).

As a judge, Samson led the Israelites for twenty years and was a constant nuisance to the Philistines. The Philistines were desperate to find a weakness, and so they approached Deliliah, a seductress, to trick Samson into revealing the source of his strength.

He said, "If someone ties my hands with seven fresh bowstrings that have not been dried, I'll become as weak as any other man." Deliliah went and told the secret to the Philistines and when Samson was sleeping, they tied him with bowstrings. Yet when Deliliah woke him shouting, "the Philistines are here," Samson woke and snapped the bowstrings easily.

Delilah hounded Samson, begging him to divulge the source of his strength. And each time, Samson told a new story. And each time the enemy came, Samson easily broke through the trap.

But Deliliah was relentless and finally Samson revealed his strength was in his hair and that it had never been cut. So when he was asleep, Deliliah shaved his head, and the Philistines attacked and captured Samson. They gouged out his eyes and took him in chains to grind grain in Gaza. But slowly, his hair grew back.

Not long after that, three thousand Philistines gathered to celebrate and offer sacrifice to their god, Dagon. They brought out Samson to show off their captured prisoner. Samson asked the servant to put his hands on the columns of the temple. He prayed, "'Sovereign LORD, remember me. Please,

God, strengthen me just once more, and let me with one blow get revenge on the Philistines for my two eyes.' ... Then he pushed with all his might and down came the temple on the rulers and all the people it" (Judges 15:28,30). Scripture says with this one act, Samson killed more people in his death than he did in his entire life.

Throughout Samson's life, he was unpredictable, but his change happened in his final prayer for the Lord's help and strength. And in his final act, he dealt a crushing blow to the people who had been oppressing the people for decades. We are never too far gone to be used by God.

Pivot from the belief that if you're heading in the wrong direction—or perhaps have sinned grievously against the Lord—that He is done working in your life.

Pivot to the clear belief that God meets you where you are today and is fully able to forgive and begin using you again to fulfill His ongoing miracle of loving anyone who would repent and call upon His name.

Prayer
"Lord, thank You that You are the source of my strength and joy. Give me the daily strength to faithfully follow You in humility and love. Amen."

Your Pivotal Moment of Faith
Whether the pivot or change in your life comes at the beginning of your life or the end,

transformation and a relationship is the key. Make a commitment to forge some new relationships and opportunities and commit each one to the Lord as you do it.

Nehemiah: From Cupbearer to Wall Builder

"Many are the plans in a person's heart, but it is the LORD's purpose that prevails."
(Proverbs 19:21)

After the Babylonians captured Judah, they destroyed the wall around Jerusalem and raided and ruined Solomon's Temple. Then they scattered many of the Jewish people to other countries. One of those captives, Nehemiah the son of Hakaliah, held a prestigious position in the Persian kingdom of Susa as the king's cupbearer. As the cupbearer, Nehemiah sampled every drink for the king before giving it to him to prevent poisoning. He served the king with joy and a happy personality.

One day a Jewish friend, Hanani, came to Nehemiah with some Jewish survivors who had escaped from Jerusalem. With great distress, these new arrivals told Nehemiah the walls of Jerusalem were torn down and the gates to the city were burned. "When I heard these things, I sat down and wept. For some days I mourned and fasted and prayed before the God of heaven" (Nehemiah 1:4).

Because Nehemiah spoke and stood with the king, he prayed for the Lord to guide his steps and give him the right words to speak.

As Nehemiah appeared before the king, the ruler noticed the sad appearance of his cupbearer and asked, "Why is your face so sad?"

"May the King live forever. I've learned the city of my fathers is in ruin and the gates were destroyed with fire," he explained.

With a sincere look, the king asked, "What do you request?"

In silence Nehemiah uttered a quick prayer for guidance and said, "If it pleases the king and I have found favor, send me to Jerusalem to rebuild it."

The king asked for some additional details such as the length of his trip. Nehemiah requested letters of recommendation from the king, as well as wood and supplies to rebuild the broken gates and walls. The king granted Nehemiah's request and sent him to Jerusalem to rebuild. Some of the local people opposed the rebuilding but Nehemiah and the people rebuilt the wall in 52 days (Nehemiah 6:15).

Nehemiah could have stayed in his position with the king and safely done nothing with this news from Jerusalem. Instead, Nehemiah spent time in prayer and fasting, then took his request for a change to the king. The king granted his request and sent him to lead the rebuilding project along with the materials he needed for the project.

What can we learn from the example of Nehemiah? When he heard about a need, he prayed and fasted asking the Lord what he wanted him to do about the news. Then when he was in the presence of the king, he quickly prayed for guidance and asked for what God showed him in his heart.

Maybe you see a need in your family or your community. Nehemiah has insights to teach each of us about how to respond to needs that cross our path.

Pivot from feeling like you're all alone in your desire to help others build or rebuild a strong relationship with God.

Pivot to the firm reliance on God that it's His desire for everyone in your sphere of influence to have the firm protection and care from the God who sent His only Son to forgive sins, and who is able to both build—and rebuild—a wall of faith that God is able to do all that He has promised.

Prayer
"Father, I understand that I can't change everything that crosses my path but give me a sensitive heart to listen to You and Your Words. Guide my steps in ways that I can't see at the moment. In Jesus' name. Amen."

Your Pivotal Moment of Faith
In the space below or in a journal, write down the name of one person you know who needs to build their wall of faith, and one person who needs to rebuild that wall. You can't save the whole world, that's God's job. But you can pray, and when the time is right, help them work through whatever questions or issues they might have.

Simeon: From Patiently Waiting . . . to Fulfillment

"Wait for the LORD; be strong and take heart and wait for the LORD." (Psalm 27:14)

The Gospel of Luke begins with the story of the birth of Jesus. Caesar Augustus had decreed that everyone had to return to their hometown and register for the census. Joseph and his pregnant wife, Mary, traveled to Bethlehem from Nazareth, a distance of about ninety miles over rough terrain, and stayed in a stable because there was no room in the inn. The shepherds came to the stable because the angels declared to them that the Messiah had been born. Then Luke includes an often forgotten story about a devout man in Jerusalem named Simeon.

According to Hebrew law, parents had to bring their child to the temple in Jerusalem to be circumcised eight days after the birth. Joseph brought Mary and Jesus to the temple for this dedication. When he was younger the Holy Spirit revealed to the righteous and devout Simeon, that he would not die before he saw the Lord's Christ. Through the years, Simeon had been waiting patiently in the temple for the fulfilment of the prophecy. It was not easy to wait but day after day, Simeon came to the temple in daily prayer and expectation to one day see the Christ child. As parents brought their babies into the temple, Simeon looked at each one with anticipation and listened to the Lord. Silence.

Then one day Simeon saw Joseph and Mary and his eyes fell upon the newborn in Mary's arms. In his heart, the Holy Spirit whispered to him, "This child is the One." The old man reached out to Mary and took Jesus in his arms, praised God and said, "Sovereign Lord, as you have promised, you may now dismiss your servant in peace. For my eyes have seen your salvation, which you have prepared in the sight of all nations: a light for revelation to the Gentiles, and the glory of your people Israel" (Luke 2:29-32).

While Joseph and Mary knew Jesus was there for the Jewish people, these prophetic words from Simeon also revealed their son would touch the entire world. The parents marveled at this revelation about their small son.

The Gospel of Luke adds one more detail about this exchange. Simeon blessed the parents and said to Mary, "This child is destined to cause the falling and rising of many in Israel, and to be a sign that will be spoken against, so that the thoughts of many hearts will be revealed. And a sword will pierce your own soul too" (Luke 2:34-35). Mary kept these words from Simeon in her heart and 33 years later this young mother would gather with some other women at the foot of the cross in Golgotha where Jesus was crucified for the sins of the world.

We don't know if Simeon was patient or frustrated at having to wait so long for the Messiah. But ultimately, Simeon waited patiently for the

Holy Spirit to allow him to see the baby Jesus. And his patience was rewarded.

Pivot from "giving up" on people you've been hoping would turn their heart to the Lord.

Pivot to a "never give up" mentality when it comes to those in your world. After all, God never gave up on you but waited patiently for your own faith to mature—at just the right moment in history.

Prayer
"Lord, it is not easy to be patient but as I wait on You for what You are doing in my life—and the lives of others—give me the strength and endurance that only You can provide. In Jesus' name. Amen."

Your Pivotal Moment of Faith
God's Word is filled with promises for Christians. Take a moment and choose one of the promises of God. Write it on a card that you carry and read several times throughout the day. Celebrate God's answer, whenever you receive it.

Martha: Too Busy for Jesus?

"Serve wholeheartedly, as if you were serving the Lord, not people, because you know that the Lord will reward each one for whatever good they do, whether they are slave or free." (Ephesians 6:7-8)

Three siblings were close personal friends of Jesus Christ: Martha, Mary and Lazarus. Their home was in Bethany, which was located near Jerusalem. Jesus of Nazareth was one of the most renowned people in the area and normally attracted large crowds of people to listen to His teaching and watch His miracles of healing the sick. Because of his unpredictable schedule, Martha never knew when Jesus was going to suddenly arrive at their home.

On one occasion when Jesus arrived, Martha started cooking while her sister Mary sat at the feet of Jesus listening to His teaching.

Martha was bothered that she was busy cooking without Mary's help. She interrupted Jesus and demanded, "Lord, don't You care that Mary has left me, so I have to do all this work alone? Tell her to help me!"

In many ways, Martha ruins her own dinner party and forces her honored guest to arbitrate this sibling squabble about household duties. Jesus takes this squabble and turns it into a teaching moment. "'Martha, Martha,' the Lord answered, 'you are worried and upset about many things, but few things are needed—or indeed only one'" (Luke 10:41-42). Jesus explained that Mary had chosen to listen and that is better than cooking in the kitchen. Jesus made a decision regarding the sibling rivalry saying, "Mary's choice will not be taken away from her."

While Martha's diligence in serving was admirable, Jesus could see she was leaving the best out of her day. It's always a "heart" thing with Jesus. Our actions can look noble, but they're often just a cover-up for resentment or fear of not having everything "just right." Are you tempted to DO for Jesus more than BE with Jesus? If so, you have some Martha tendencies that Jesus will want you to address. If you're a "doer," list a few ways below how you might recognize this tendency and pursue "being" with Jesus with a bit more diligence. Whether it's mindless distractions like "Tik Tok" or "reels," or big distractions like a need to have things "perfect" to fill your need to look good to others, start by making one change that will give you more time to sit at the feet of Jesus.

Pivot from the daily "do list" that squeezes out time with Jesus.

Pivot to building a regular habit of listening to God through contemplative prayer and a consistent time in the Scriptures to hear what God might say to you that day.

Prayer
"Lord, thank You for these insights that You taught Martha about choices on what is truly

important—listening to Jesus. Help me to make better choices with my time and day. In Jesus' name. Amen."

Your Pivotal Moment of Faith

Without being overly obsessed with daily times with God, discover what rhythms in your life should be altered to give you more time to hear from God on a frequent basis.

Bathsheba: From Tragedy to Prominence

"I will repay you for the years the locusts have eaten—the great locust and the young locust, the other locusts and the locust swarm—my great army that I sent among you." (Joel 2:25)

Second Samuel 11 is where we first meet Bathsheba. One evening, King David wandered outside his palace. The bulk of the men in his kingdom were off at war. Feeling bored, David looked across the city of Jerusalem. To his surprise on one of the rooftops, he saw a beautiful woman bathing. The king was captivated by this woman's beauty. In fact, David called one of his trusted servants and said, "See that woman on that rooftop? Learn what you can about her." The servant discovered her name was Bathsheba and that among other things, she was married to a man named Uriah, a soldier in David's army. King David asked to see her, and he took her into his bedroom as if she was his wife.

A few weeks later, Bathsheba sent a message to David saying she was pregnant. He immediately created a plan to cover up his affair. Because Bathsheba's husband Uriah was on the battlefield with the other men, David sent a message to his commander Joab and asked that Uriah return to Jerusalem. The king assumed Uriah would return and have sexual relations with his wife. But Uriah acted with integrity and refused to return home to his wife while his men were on the battlefield. Finally, King David released Uriah to return to the war. But he sent a message with the soldier for his commander Joab. "Put Uriah on the front line then pull back so he is killed." Joab carried out his King's wishes. As expected, Uriah died. After a period of mourning, Bathsheba became one of King David's wives.

After the baby was born, he became ill, and the prophet Nathan revealed God's displeasure about David's affair and the murder of Uriah. The prophet declared that the baby would die. In an effort to save the sick child, David fasted and pleaded with God. None of David's actions changed the situation, and the baby died. Afterwards, David comforted Bathsheba, and she got pregnant again with a second son, whom they named Solomon. Bathsheba and David's second son became the wisest man who ever lived.

Because of King David's affair, Bathsheba lost her husband and because of David's sin, they lost a firstborn son. Despite her tragic past, Bathsheba is one of five women who are honored in the family tree of Jesus Christ (see Matthew 1).

Your own sins—and likely the sins of others—have marred your life in some way. But God is constantly in the business of restoring failures and turning ashes to gold. Determine today that despite whatever has happened in your past, God can create something beautiful.

Pivot from the belief that even grievous sin will separate you or others from a strong relationship with God.

Pivot to dependence on the grace and love of God to redeem any bad choices you've made, or that others have made that affects your life.

Prayer
"Lord, thank You that don't hold my past—or future—sins against me. Through the blood of Jesus, I am forgiven. And thank You that You can restore my future and make it bright, even beyond a past that failed to honor who You are and what You've done for me. In Your name. Amen."

Your Pivotal Moment of Faith
Write down at least five circumstances from your life when the Lord transformed past failures and helped you to create a bright future. Remembering God's faithfulness to make sense out of past issues is essential when future mistakes try to tear you down.

Naomi: Finding the Courage to Go Forward

"Have I not commanded you? Be strong and courageous. Do not be afraid; do not be discouraged, for the Lord your God will be with you wherever you go." (Joshua 1:9)

When a severe famine struck the land of Israel, for their own survival, some of the families in Bethlehem of Judah fled to Moab. This included Naomi's husband Elimelech and his wife Naomi along with their two sons, Mahlon and Killion. While living in Moab, Elimelech grew ill and died. Thankfully Naomi's family grew when her sons met and married two Moabite women, Orpah and Ruth. While in Moab, tragedy struck the family again and both sons died.

Suffering heartbreak with her loss, Naomi mustered the courage to press on. Then the news reached Naomi that God was blessing Bethlehem again. The famine was over, and once more, bountiful crops were growing. Naomi and her two daughters-in-law decided to return to Judah. The trio packed their belongings and began to travel toward Israel. While on the road, Naomi came to the conclusion that she was perhaps holding the two women back from having a great life. So she released the two Moabite women of any obligation to her and encouraged them to return to their families, get remarried and begin a new chapter in their lives. This step of faith by Naomi—trading companionship for what could have been a lonely life—could not have been an easy decision. The result? For Orpah, Naomi's advice seemed sound, and she hugged her mother-in-law and began her return to Moab. Ruth made a different choice saying, "No, Naomi, I will go with you and your people will be my people."

When the two women arrived in Bethlehem, their old friends were delighted to see Naomi again but grieved the loss of her husband and two sons in Moab. Even through her pain, and her unselfish desire for her daughter's in law to have a fuller life--God's hand was still on Naomi's life.

During the barley harvest, like others who were poor, Ruth gleaned some barley on the edges of the field. One day Ruth returned to Naomi with an excess of grain. "Where were you today, Ruth?" Naomi asked. Ruth explained she had met a generous man named Boaz. In recognition of God's guiding hand on Ruth, Naomi told her that Boaz was a relative of Elimelech. Then Naomi told Ruth what she needed to do to marry Boaz and Ruth followed her instructions. After Ruth and Boaz were married, they had a son named Obed. Through her care for Obed like her own son, Naomi experienced God's restoration and blessing. The Moabite Ruth became the grandmother of one of the greatest kings in Israel, David. In the midst of tragedy, Naomi continued trusting God's orchestration of her life.

As we face challenges, you can embrace faith with courage like Naomi and trust your future will be beyond anything you can imagine.

Pivot from believing that God has lost your file and that He no longer cares for the details of your life.

Pivot to the joy that complete surrender to God's ability to create good out of even the worst circumstances can give you the peace you need to move forward in anticipation of better things ahead.

Prayer
"God, thank You for how You restored Naomi after her tragedy. Teach me these lessons of faith and help me to trust Your guiding hand in the challenges that life gives. In the name of Jesus. Amen."

Your Pivotal Moment of Faith
List a tragic circumstance in your life that in hindsight you can see how God used as a blessing for your soul.

Jochebed: Faith that Freed a Nation

"It is for freedom that Christ has set us free. Stand firm, then, and do not let yourselves be burdened again by a yoke of slavery." (Galatians 5:1)

Among the pregnant Hebrew women, the news spread like wildfire. To control the ever-expanding population of the Hebrew slaves in Egypt Pharoah had called all of the Hebrew midwives to his palace and told them, "During a childbirth, I command you to check the gender of every new baby and if it is a male, kill those babies." The command sent a stab of fear through the midwives and pregnant Hebrew women. They wondered how to disobey Pharoah and to follow their Creator God who cherished life.

Then one of the midwives had an idea for the others, "Let's tell Pharoah the Hebrew women are different and too quick with their childbirth and they are done before we even arrive" (see Exodus 1:19).

The Lord was watching over one pregnant Hebrew woman in particular who was named Jochebed. When she had her baby, it was a male and for three months she was careful to hide the child. As the baby grew, this deception was harder to carry out because of the child's loud crying. So, Jochebed made a cradle basket of reeds and sealed the bottom and sides to make it waterproof. With a prayer for God's protection, she arranged her baby in the basket. Jochebed gently lifted her baby's basket cradle and put it into the Nile River. She then stationed her oldest daughter, Miriam, to watch her baby brother. Then the basket floated near where Pharoah's daughter regularly bathed in the Nile.

Pharoah's daughter noticed the crying baby in the cradle. She lifted the child into her arms. Miriam came forward to Pharoah's daughter and asked, "Do you need a nurse maid for this child? I know someone who can help you?"

"Yes, please bring this nurse maid to me." Miriam went to her mother, Jochebed and Pharoah's daughter assigned her and even paid her to nurse her baby! God was answering her prayer of protection for her son in an unexpected way. Later Pharoah's daughter adopted the child and named him, "Moses," from the Hebrew term to draw out because the daughter drew Moses out of the water. What Jochebed couldn't have known then were the amazing plans God had in store for her son and how they would benefit the Jewish nation.

In Hebrews 11, heroes who show courageous faith are recognized and Jochebed is one of those few people. She protected the life of Moses and knew her baby was no ordinary child. Her courage and love for her child and faith in the God of the Universe paved the way for Moses to lead the entire Hebrew nation from the bondage of slavery in Egypt to freedom. Also, Jochebed's story is a practical example of how God's continued guidance and direction is in our daily life whether we are conscious of it or not.

Pivot from despair when earthly circumstances might tend to capture your spirit and hold it hostage to fear.

Pivot to belief in a present and loving God who consistently shows up—right on time as only He can do—to provide hope, answers and purpose to situations the world might call "hopeless."

Prayer
"Lord, thank You for Jochebed and her courageous faith in You to protect her son. Help me to be more aware of your guidance and how You are leading my life day in and day out. In the name of Jesus, Amen."

Your Pivotal Moment of Faith
Take a few moments and consider how God is ordering the steps in your life and move forward in faith and courage.

Titus: Leading with Integrity

"May integrity and uprightness protect me, because my hope, LORD, is in you." (Psalm 25:21)

One of the Gentiles who converted to Christianity was a man named Titus. He served as one of the apostle Paul's trusted assistants. The Scriptures tell us very little about this man of God, but from the few references we have to him, and the nature of Paul's epistle to him, we gain a picture of a man dedicated to serving the Lord.

The first mention of Titus is in the book of Galatians where he is a companion for Paul and Barnabas. A trusted member of Paul's team, Titus pivoted from his role as a secretary for Paul to a position of leadership. He went to Corinth and was charged with dealing with a difficult church situation which needed strong leadership and diplomacy.

Years later, after Paul's first trial in Rome and his subsequent release, Paul left Titus on the island of Crete so he could establish a church there. While Titus led the church in Crete, the Apostle Paul wrote him the letter which became the Epistle to Titus. Paul gave Titus some detailed advice about how to select church leaders along with also encouraging him to model and teach godly behavior. Then Paul asked Titus to travel to the city of Nicopolis (Titus 3:12) which is located on the western coast of modern-day Greece where

Paul hoped to spend the winter. Later, before Paul was killed in Rome, he wrote that Titus had gone to the province of Dalmatia (2 Timothy 4:10), probably to minister the Good News there. According to tradition, Titus settled in Crete and served as the bishop of the church there until he died at an old age.

Throughout his life, Titus traveled with Paul and served with integrity and consistency to spread the Gospel message to others. As a trusted member of Paul's team, Titus serves as an example of the type of service we can do in the church.

Pivot from the feeling you may be "past your prime," or "not qualified" to serve the LORD in the service of others.

Pivot to the fact that God does indeed empower anyone willing to be used by the Spirit to do good here on earth. Everyone has been given gifts and those gifts, combined with a humble dependence on God's will, allows Kingdom-oriented believers to accomplish Kingdom business.

Prayer
"God, thank You for the example of Titus and his faithful service to the cause of Christ, which he accomplished with integrity. Help me to learn from his example and follow Christ with integrity and faithfulness. In the powerful name of Jesus. Amen."

Your Pivotal Moment of Faith
None of us know what lies ahead for us in our ministry but what actions can you take today to prepare for serving others with integrity?

Ehud: God Uses Unlikely People

"But God chose the foolish things of the world to shame the wise; God chose the weak things of the world to shame the strong." (1 Corinthians 1:27)

The people in Israel had grown apathetic and distant from the God who rescued them from Egypt. As Judges 3:12 says "Again the Israelites did evil in the eyes of the LORD, and because they did this evil the LORD gave Eglon king of Moab power over Israel." For 18 years Eglon King of Moab controlled the lives of the Jewish people. The people cried out to the Lord and an unlikely man, Ehud, from the tribe of Benjamin, came to their rescue.

The Bible tells us that Ehud was left-handed. Because it raises this small but important detail, some translators wonder if Ehud was actually handicapped in his right hand. Regardless, Ehud could only use his left hand and not his right hand.

The Israelites sent Ehud to bring their tribute payment to King Eglon. In preparation, Ehud took a double-edged sword about 18 inches long and strapped it to his right thigh under his clothing. Since a right-handed man would have hidden a sword on his left side, Ehud's blade went unnoticed by the guards.

Ehud presented the tribute to King Eglon, then said that he had a secret message for the king's ears only.

King Eglon was intrigued and dismissed his attendants saying, "Leave us." After the servants left the room, only the king remained in the room with Ehud.

Ehud came toward the king and said, "I have a message for you from God." At these words, King Eglon began to stand up from his seat. Ehud reached across to his right thigh, grabbed the sword and stuck the entire sword including the handle into the belly of the obese king.

Leaving the sword, Ehud closed the doors of the upper room and locked them. Then he went out on the porch of the upper room and climbed down the outside of the palace and left the ground. Because the king had ordered privacy, his body wasn't discovered until long after Ehud had escaped.

When Ehud reached Seriah, he blew a trumpet and called the Israelites to him saying, "Follow me." Ehud led them to the fords of the Jordan, and they killed ten thousand Moabites. No one escaped and the land had peace from the Moabites for the next 80 years (Judges 3:30).

This is certainly not a children's bedtime story—and even more certainly not a call to action against anyone alive in your world—but God had a purpose: to do what was needed to save his people from an evil leader. He chose to use someone who most definitely could have been handicapped. The truth is God rarely uses the perfect of the world to do His will here on earth. He uses all of us, warts and handicaps and all. When you become self-aware enough to realize this fact, God can and will use you to accomplish something you didn't see coming.

Pivot from the belief that God only requires whole and healthy people to serve Him.

Pivot to the knowledge that just as you are, you can be used by God in the situations He has—in His wisdom—placed you in.

Prayer
"Father, I give my life to You and ask You to use me today. It may be in unexpected ways like You have used others. Direct my steps through Your Holy Spirit. In the name of Jesus. Amen"

Your Pivotal Moment of Faith
Do you have an unexpected strength that people don't know about? How can the Lord use this strength for His Glory. Let your imagination roam.

Peter: Faith-Building Walking on the Water

"Come, follow Me," Jesus said, "and I will make you fishers of men."
(Matthew 4:19 Berean Study Bible)

When Jesus began His three years of public ministry, He started by preaching the Gospel of the Kingdom of God on the shore of the Lake of Gennesaret to a small but eager crowd. There were two boats and Jesus climbed into the boat that belonged to Simon and said, "Let's go out from the shore." They moved the boat away from the shore and Jesus taught the crowd from there.

When He finished speaking, Jesus told Simon, "Move out into the deep water and cast out your nets for some fish."

Looking skeptical, Simon Peter said, "Master, we've been fishing hard all night and didn't catch anything. But because you have asked, we will try it." Soon the nets were filled with fish and Simon and his partners had to signal another boat to help them haul the catch into shore. When they reached the shore, Simon fell to his knees saying, "Go away from me, Lord, for I am a sinful man!" (Luke 5:8).

After Simon and his partners James and John brought their fish and boats to the shore, that's when Jesus challenged them, "Follow me and you will catch men instead of fish." They left their boats and fish to follow Jesus.

As Jesus ministered throughout Israel, Peter became a committed disciple and a personal witness of the miracles that Jesus performed for different people. One indelible lesson occurred when Jesus left to pray alone on the mountainside as His disciples took the boat across the Sea of Galilee. As their boat tossed and turned in the waves, the men feared the worst. Suddenly, they saw Jesus. When they first saw Him walking on the water, they were terrified and believed He was a ghost. But Jesus calmed their fears telling them to take courage and not be afraid.

Peter spoke up and said, "Lord, if it's You, I'd like to also walk on the water. Tell me to come to You."

Jesus invited Peter to come toward Him. Walking on water must have been scary to this lifelong fisherman. Yet with the permission and encouragement of Jesus, Peter climbed out of the boat and walked toward Him. Suddenly, Peter noticed the wind, became afraid, and then began to sink into the water and cried out, "Lord, save me!"

Immediately Jesus reached out His hand and caught him. "You of little faith," He said, "why did you doubt?" And when they climbed into the boat, the wind died down (Matthew 14:27-32). The disciples were amazed at this demonstration from Jesus that He could control the wind and the sea. The experience affirmed to the disciples that Jesus was the Christ and Son of God.

As a follower of Jesus, it's easy to be fearful instead of trusting. What fears are you facing today as you consider the challenge of "fishing for men" that Jesus has given His followers? Is a friend or customer hurting and you're wondering whether Jesus might be their answer? Or possibly the church has asked you to lead a small group and that's a bit outside your comfort zone? Whatever fear you are facing, follow the example of Peter walking on the water with Jesus. Take the first step, and know that He is always there to catch you should you feel you're in too deep.

Pivot from the fear of being used as God's instrument to become a fisher of men.

Pivot to the realization that every action we take to help another soul on their path fulfills the call to make disciples.

Prayer
"Lord, turn my fears into steps of faith and opportunities to trust and follow You. Guide me and use me to share my faith with others who cross my path today. In Your Name, Amen."

Your Pivotal Moment of Faith
Often Christians believe that sharing our faith is something for the professionals like a pastor or Bible teacher. In fact, the Scriptures encourage every believer to let the light of their faith-walk to shine and draw others to a relationship with Jesus. What one thing might you do this week to live or share the Good News with someone in your life?

Noah: The Long Path of Obedience

"Therefore, everyone who hears these words of mine and puts them into practice is like a wise man who built his house on the rock."
(Matthew 7:24)

During the days when Noah walked the earth, and even before, some men lived for hundreds of years. From the opening chapters of Genesis, we learn that the Creator God knows the hearts and minds of every single person. When God called Adam and Eve in the garden when they tried to hide after disobeying God's one command, He knew where they were. When He asked Cain about the location of Abel the Lord didn't need an answer to His question. He already knew. And as Adam and Eve's family grew and began filling the earth, sin began spreading as well.

When God saw the wickedness and how it had spread throughout humanity and all the evil that was in their hearts, "The LORD regretted that he had made human beings on the earth, and his heart was deeply troubled. So, the LORD said, 'I will wipe from the face of the earth the human race I have created—and with them the animals, the birds and the creatures that move along the ground—for I regret that I have made them'" (Genesis 6:6-7).

Across the multitude of humanity, only one person stood out—Noah, who lived in fellowship with God.

When God told Noah to build an ark, he was about 550 years old. Instead of farming or selling flood insurance, Noah changed his life and followed God's direction. The Lord told Noah to make the ark 450 feet long, 75 feet wide and 45 feet high. (Genesis 6:15). He built it with multiple rooms from cypress wood and coated it with pitch to make it waterproof on the inside and out. This massive structure took Noah about forty to fifty years to build. The people around Noah must have believed his actions were crazy. Why would anyone build such a structure on dry land away from any body of water? What purpose could it possibly serve? Despite any mocking he may have received, Noah built the ark that God had commanded.

Then God asked Noah to collect a male and female of every kind of creature, along with food for them, and load it all into the ark. God forewarned Noah that He was preparing for forty days and nights of rain. Each command Noah completed. Then, with his whole family, Noah, at 600 years of age, entered the ark and God shut the door behind him. Then the sky opened, and it began to rain. Eventually the whole earth flooded, but the ark floated safely on top of the water. Finally, the rain stopped, and after another year of floating, the ark came to rest on dry ground. After the ark was emptied, God gave a rainbow as a promise to show He would never destroy the earth again by a flood.

Has God led you in an unexpected direction with your job, family, or relationships? It may not be the expected path, but God is asking for our obedience to His direction and leading.

Pivot from the need to take total control of your life, separate and apart from relying on God.

Pivot to finding ways to include God, His Holy Spirit as well as other godly people in your life to help discern His will in all of your major life decisions.

Prayer
"God, as we read the Bible, direct our lives so we put Scripture into practice. In the name of Jesus. Amen."

Your Pivotal Moment of Faith
Consider a time in your life where God directed you to take an unexpected action. How did it turn out for you? Celebrate God's direction and guidance in your everyday life.

Philip: The Spirit-Guided Evangelist

"But you will receive power when the Holy Spirit comes on you; and you will be my witnesses in Jerusalem, and in all Judea and Samaria, and to the ends of the earth." (Acts 1:8)

The Book of Acts gives the inspiring story of how the Good News about Jesus spread from Jerusalem to Samaria and to the other parts of the world. As Christians faced persecution in Jerusalem—where Stephen was martyred for his faith—the message soon spread to Samaria. Philip, one of the early leaders of the church preached the Gospel but with more than words; he also was a conduit for God's miracles. As Acts 8:6-8 says, "When the crowds heard Philip and saw the signs he performed, they all paid close attention to what he said. For with shrieks, impure spirits came out of many, and many who were paralyzed or lame were healed. So there was great joy in that city." These miracles drew crowds to come listen to the message about Jesus. Philip was having a great ministry in Samaria, but then the Lord called him to another place for his ministry, and in obedience, Philip went.

An angel of the Lord told Philip to go to the desert and walk along the road from Jerusalem to Gaza. An Ethiopian eunuch, a man of prestige and position in charge of the queen's treasury, was traveling in a chariot to Jerusalem to worship. The

Spirit told Philip, "Go near and overtake this chariot."

As the evangelist got near to the Ethiopian, he could hear that he was reading Isaiah aloud. Philip asked, "Do you understand what you are reading?"

Shaking his head no, the Ethiopian eunuch said, "How could I understand these words unless someone explains the meaning?" Then he motioned for Philip to come into his chariot and look at the words from Isaiah on the scroll. He was reading from Isaiah 53, "'He was led like a sheep to the slaughter, and as a lamb before its shearer is silent, so he did not open his mouth. In his humiliation he was deprived of justice. Who can speak of his descendants? For his life was taken from the earth'" (Acts 8:32-33).

The eunuch asked Philip, "Was the prophet talking about himself or someone else?" Philip began to speak with this leader about the recent death and resurrection of Jesus Christ. As they went down the road in the chariot, they came to a body of water and the eunuch asked, "What prevents me from being baptized?"

"You may be baptized if you believe with all your heart."

"He answered, I believe Jesus Christ is the Son of God." They stopped the chariot and Philip baptized the man. When he came out of the water, the Spirit of God suddenly moved Philip to a different location, and the eunuch left rejoicing at his changed life.

Notice Philip was open to God's divine direction in his life, and he took action with this direction. It's an example for us to follow with our lives.

Pivot from the belief that God is incapable of directing your path into the lives of others so you can deliver a message of hope.

Pivot to a faith that might contain a bit more wonder and mystery about how God works; staying open to His leading when you come in contact with a world God loves.

Prayer
"Lord when I read the Bible, direct my heart and plans for the day. Direct my steps through the power of the Holy Spirit as You did for Philip the Evangelist. In Jesus' name. Amen."

Your Pivotal Moment of Faith
For the next seven days, stay open and anticipate that God may lead you into the path of someone who needs His supernatural touch. Write down your experiences so you'll remember how God can use you.

John the Baptist: Was He Worthy of Jesus?

"The next day John saw Jesus coming toward him and said, 'Look, the Lamb of God, who takes away the sin of the world!'" (John 1:29)

Jerusalem and the surrounding cities were buzzing with conversation and excitement. A strange man named John, who wore camel-hair clothing and ate wild honey was preaching at the Jordan River. Many of the older people in the Jewish community may have recalled John's parents Zechariah and Elizabeth and the circumstances surrounding John's birth.

John's parents were well-past child-bearing age. One day, in his service as a priest, Zechariah went into the Holy of Holies of the Temple and saw an angel who told him, "Your wife will be pregnant with a son that you will name John." Just as the angel foretold, soon a baby was born to this elderly couple, and they named him John. From his unusual birth, people knew John was on a different path in life.

Now his preaching stirred controversy among the Pharisees and the Sadducees. John spoke like a teacher with authority even though he had never been formally schooled in the Jewish laws. He told the people, "Repent of your sins and turn to God because the Kingdom of Heaven is near."

As John's message spread, large crowds gathered and listened to him. As a public sign of their decision to change and follow God, John encouraged those in the crowd to be baptized in the Jordan River. When asked who he was, John made clear, "I am not the Messiah, but someone is coming soon, and I am not worthy to even untie his sandals."

One day, John saw Jesus waiting for John to baptize Him. When it was Jesus' turn, John began to protest saying, "I can't baptize you. You should be baptizing me." Jesus cut John off, explaining that God wanted John to baptize Him. So, John stood with Jesus in the water and baptized Him. As Jesus came up out of the water, John heard a voice from Heaven saying, "This is my Beloved Son. Listen to Him."

Even in biblical times, people felt like they didn't deserve to serve Jesus—even John the Baptist. The Bible is full of truth about how God really thinks about us, like this passage, "While we were yet sinners, Christ died for us" (Romans 5:8) It's a familiar truth echoed and amplified throughout the New Testament.

You *are* worthy to serve Jesus, no matter what you've done or how you feel.

Pivot from any beliefs that even in your sinful state as a human on planet earth that you're unworthy to serve the Lord.

Pivot to not just believing that about you, but also about those whose life and actions are far away from God. They're worthy, too, and need to be treated as the unique creation of God that they are.

Prayer

"Lord, help me to know and feel that You believe I am worthy—and that everyone I see in my own little world is worthy, as well. In Your Name. Amen."

Your Pivotal Moment of Faith

Look for one person in your sphere of influence who has their countenance down. Look for ways to let them know how special they are to you . . . and to God.

Sarah: Laughing at God's Promise

"I will make you into a great nation and I will bless you; I will make your name great, and you will be a blessing." (Genesis 12:2)

God made a promise to Abram when he was 75 years old and his wife Sarai was 65 years old that a son would be born to them. Both of them were well past the child-bearing age. For ten years they waited for God's to fulfill His promise. When nothing happened, Sarai gave her Egyptian maid Hagar to Abram and she bore Ishmael. This only caused trouble in the family. Ishmael was not the son God has promised.

On four different occasions in the Genesis, the Lord physically appeared to Abram. On the third occasion, Abram was 100 years old, and Sarai was 90. On this occasion He changed Abram's name to Abraham, Father of Many, and Sarai to Sarah (which means laughing). Again, God promised Abraham a son and this time confirmed that it would be a son born to Sarah and that his name was to be Isaac.

Sometime later, God came down from heaven again and appeared to Abraham by the trees at Mamre. During this visit, the Lord said, "I will surely return to you about this time next year, and Sarah your wife will have a son" (Genesis 18:10). In her tent, Sarah was listening to the conversation. As an elderly woman, the idea for her to have a child sounded ridiculous and she laughed to herself. Then God asked Abraham, "Why did Sarah laugh? Is anything too hard for the Lord?"

Yet just as God had promised, Sarah had a son, Isaac, after 25 long years of waiting. Despite her earlier mistake with Hagar, Sarah faithfully stood by Abraham and ultimately trusted that God would fulfill His promise. Sarah's faith made her a pivotal figure in the Bible as God fulfilled his covenant with Abraham. Eventually the descendants of Abraham would be more numerous than the stars in the sky (Genesis 22:17).

The Lord's promise of a child to Sarah and Abraham took years to fulfill. As we pray and ask God to use us in the lives of others, are we expecting instant answers or are we faithful for the long haul of life? Whether solving a situation in your own life or helping a loved one—whether a family member or friend—remember to be patient. And pray for that same patience as you pray for others.

Pivot from believing that God doesn't answer prayer if it doesn't happen right away.

Pivot to a long journey viewpoint of life. Even if it takes years, realize that God knows the perfect time to change someone's life—including your own.

Prayer
"Lord of all the universe, if I'm honest I often do not have the patience to wait for your answers.

Help me to trust You for each day and each life situation. Amen"

Your Pivotal Moment of Faith

Notice the years of patient and faithful following from Abraham and Sarah until God brought about His promise. Write down three prayer requests that you anticipate may take many years to be answered. Set your mind and prayers for the long haul and don't lose heart that God will answer.

Aaron: From the First High Priest to Failure with the People

"You shall have no other gods before me."
(Exodus 20:3)

After many years in Egypt, Aaron was now traveling to the desert of Midian looking for his younger brother, Moses. He didn't know why he needed to meet with Moses, all he knew is that God had told him, "'Go into the wilderness to meet Moses'" (Exodus 4:27). To his surprise, when they were reunited, Aaron found that his brother had been expecting him. Moses explained to Aaron about the mission God had given them and they set off for Egypt.

The brothers approached Pharaoh demanding the release of the Hebrew slaves, but Pharaoh refused. So God sent a series of plagues upon Egypt, each worse than the last. But each time Pharoah hardened his heart and refused to listen to Moses and Aaron. The final plague was the worst. "At midnight the LORD struck down all the firstborn in Egypt, from the firstborn of Pharaoh...to the firstborn of the prisoner." (Exodus 12:29). Pharoah relented and let the Israelites leave. Though he tried one last time to keep hold of the Hebrews, his armies were swallowed by the Red Sea.

Soon thereafter, God called Moses to go up on Mount Siani to receive the Ten Commandments. But after Moses had been away for a while, the people grew restless. They turned to Aaron who told the people to bring him all their gold. Using this gold, Aaron fashioned a golden calf and declared it to be a god. The people rejoiced. But when Moses returned, a righteous anger burned within him and the people were severely punished. Aaron could only watch as many died for his failure in declaring a false God.

In addition to the Ten Commandments Moses received from God, he also received many detailed instructions about how the Israelites were to order their society and live their lives. As part of this, God gave specific instructions to anoint Aaron to become the high priest to lead the people in their worship as God. As High Priest it was Aaron's responsibility to perform the sacrifices and rituals required to cleanse the sins of Israel. A responsibility that would stay in his family until Jesus died to cleanse the sins of the world with one final sacrifice.

We live in a far different world than Aaron and Moses, instead of a golden calf, we have other idols in our life such as money, possessions, work, pleasure, sex, or even eating or drinking to excess. Each of these idols can steal our hearts and lives from faithfully following our first love, the Lord God.

Like all of us, Aaron wasn't perfect or sinless as he attempted to follow the Lord. But he did learn to repent of his wrongdoings and find forgiveness for his past actions. And God used him in mighty ways despite his failures. His story shows us the loving patience that God has with all of us.

Pivot from distractions that dull your vision of God's love and work in your life.

Pivot to a life that is fully aware of how distractions push your faith down, and one where these distractions get a firm "no" as you seek to make wise choices that grow your faith and the faith of others.

Prayer
"God, forgive me for following idols and falling away from You. Draw me back to You and Your Word. Thank You that You provide a way of forgiveness through the death and blood of Jesus Christ. In the Holy Name of Jesus, I pray. Amen."

Your Pivotal Moment of Faith
Consider any idols—distractions—in your life that are pulling your mind and heart away from following the Lord. Ask for forgiveness and think of three changes you could make to help make you less distracted.

Lot: Leaving Sodom and Saving His Family

"The way of fools seems right to them, but the wise listen to advice." (Proverb 12:15)

When God called Abram and his family to go to the land of Canaan, he took his family including his nephew Lot. During the journey with their families and livestock, their possessions and wealth grew until Abram's herdsmen and Lot's herdsmen were arguing over the land. So Abram said to his nephew, "There is enough land for both of us, let's split. If you go right, I'll go left. If you go left, I'll go right."

Lot looked up and could see the plain of Jordan and the lush valley surrounding Sodom and Gomorrah and chose it for himself. Yet while the vegetation of Sodom was rich and lush, the Bible includes this ominous description of its inhabitants: "Now the people of Sodom were wicked and were sinning greatly against the LORD" (Genesis 13:13).

About twenty years later, a visiting angel came to Abraham and warned him that God was about to destroy Sodom and Gomorrah. Abraham pleaded with the angel to spare the cities, and the angel finally agreed that if even ten righteous men could be found in Sodom, it would be spared (see Genesis 18:16-33).

But Sodom was already too far gone. Even still, God didn't forget about Lot. In the next chapter, the angels travel to Sodom to warn Lot about the impending destruction of the city. He was told to flee to the mountains. Lot hesitated at first, but the angels pulled him, his wife and daughters out of the city and told them to run and not look back.

The mountains looked too imposing and far away to lot, so the angels agreed to let him and his family flee to the neighboring town of Zoar. "But flee there quickly, because I cannot do anything until you reach it" (Genesis 19:22). Lot, his wife and his daughters ran towards the village, and no sooner had they arrived than God rained sulfur from the sky and destroyed Sodom and Gomorrah. But Lot's wife looked back and instantly turned into a pillar of salt. But Lot and his daughters were safe.

Did Lot know the reputation of the people Sodom when he chose to settle there? It's hard to say, but he can't have been there long before their wickedness became apparent. But in His grace, God remembered Lot and pulled him and his family out of Sodom before it faced a fiery judgment.

We all make dozens of choices every day, some good, some bad. But God has given us grace so we don't have to carry the weight of our sins ourselves. Knowing that Jesus bore those sins—even the ones only we and God know about—is hugely comforting.

Pivot from feeling condemned for sins you committed and condemning others for their sins.

Pivot to a life of freedom in Christ from our sins that we know we can't ever fix. And then extend that grace and freedom to others as they're finding their own way.

Prayer
"Lord as You direct the steps of my life, give me ears to listen and the courage to respond to your direction. And when I don't, be merciful to me, a sinner. And help me move forward like Lot and not look back with reluctance like Lot's wife. In Your Holy name. Amen."

Your Pivotal Moment of Faith
Think on a mistake—or a series of mistakes—you've made in your life. Looking back on them with any fondness leads to a death of sorts. Death to experiencing the grace of God, death to living fully today, death to having a tomorrow free from your past. While we must learn from those mistakes, we are not strong enough to carry them. That's Jesus' job. Let Him carry that past so you can truly live today.

Jairus A Father's Love for His Daughter

"'Have faith in God,' Jesus answered. 'Truly I tell you, if anyone says to this mountain, "Go, throw yourself into the sea," and does not doubt in their heart but believes that what they say will happen, it will be done for them.'" (Mark 11:22-23)

A lot of Jesus' ministry was centered around the Sea of Galilee and the settlements that surrounded it. And so it was not uncommon for Jesus and the disciples to find a crowd waiting for them when they pulled up on shore. The day recorded in Mark 5 was no different.

Among those in the crowd was one of the local synagogue leaders, Jarius. Seeing Jesus Jairus fell at His feet of Jesus pleading, "Master, my little girl is dying. Please come and lay your hands on her so she will live."

Jesus agreed to go with Jairus to see his daughter. A large crowd surrounded Jesus as He followed Jairus. Within the crowd was a woman who had suffered twelve years of bleeding that the doctors could not cure. "If I just touch His clothes," she thought, "I'll be healed." Getting close, she reached out and touched Jesus' cloak and was healed. Jesus stopped and asked, "Who touched me?" because He could feel His healing power leave him. The woman, trembling with fear, told Jesus what she had done. Jesus said, "Your faith has healed you. Go in peace and be freed from your suffering" (Mark 5:34).

While all of this was happening, some friends of Jairus arrived and said, "It's too late, Jairus. Don't trouble Jesus any longer. Your daughter is dead."

Overhearing, Jesus told Jairus, "Don't be afraid. Just believe." Arriving at the house, Jesus found many people crying about the death of the young girl. Jesus said, "Why are they crying? She is sleeping." They laughed at Jesus, But He sent everyone away except her parents, and the three disciples with Him. Then, taking the little girl's hand He, "Get up." Immediately the twelve-year-old girl stood up and walked around. "Don't tell anyone about this," Jesus cautioned as He left, "and give her something to eat."

Jairus' faith in Jesus shows how God can work in even the most desperate of situations. Throughout the Gospels, Jesus was often sensitive to the measure of faith in those whose hearts were bent toward God. When He finds people who have faith, then miracles can happen. When Jesus couldn't find people with faith, miracles didn't come.

Whether it was Jairus or the woman who reached out in faith and was healed of her bleeding, everyone who approached Jesus had their own faith story to tell. That's what God has given us. A story to tell. A story that originates through the power of Jesus and then combines with a faith that God gives to those who would believe.

Pivot from a small faith that is not sure God can still do miracles—whether it be healing or the miracle of salvation.

Pivot to the next level of faith in your journey that believes God can do far more abundantly than we can ask or think.

Prayer
"Lord, You have said if we have faith that is the size of a mustard seed then we can move mountains. Help my faith to increase and trust You for the issues in my life, large and small. In Jesus' name."

Your Pivotal Moment of Faith
Write down five to ten stories from your life to remind yourself of times God showed up for you. These are stories you can use to share with those you know you, who need to see how God can work in someone's life.

Boaz: Loving the Destitute and Poor

"But Ruth replied, 'Don't urge me to leave you or to turn back from you. Where you go I will go, and where you stay I will stay. Your people will be my people and your God my God.'" (Ruth 1:16)

The people of Judah had been hit with famine. During these years, Elimelech and Naomi his wife moved their family from Bethlehem to Moab. While in Moab, his two sons married Moabite women Ruth and Orpah. Years later, Elimelech and his sons died in the foreign country leaving Naomi and her two daughters-in-law alone and destitute. With the famine over and the crops growing again, Naomi returned to her home with her Moabite daughter, Ruth.

When the grain was harvested, the poor could pick some of the leftovers on the edge of the crop. Ruth joined other women gathering some grain on the fields of Boaz. When he learned about Ruth, Boaz commended her for helping Naomi and instructed his workers to be generous with the grain for Ruth. That evening Ruth returned with a bountiful and unexpected harvest.

"Where were you today?" Naomi asked.

"Boaz owned these fields," Ruth said.

"The Lord has smiled on you, Ruth," Naomi exclaimed. "Boaz is a relative." Naomi explained to Ruth that Boaz was one of their relatives who could possibly pay off their debts. He was known as a kinsman-redeemer. She advised her daughter-in-law to wear a special outfit and wait until late at night when everyone lay down to sleep. "Ruth, go near to Boaz and sleep near him. Boaz will understand that you are asking him to rescue our family."

That night, Ruth followed Naomi's instructions and during the night, Boaz woke up and noticed Ruth sleeping near him. He understood that, more than just marrying Ruth, she was asking Boaz to also give Naomi an heir "Bless you, Ruth, for not going after younger men. But I have to speak with another relative who is first before I can be your kinsman-redeemer.". Boaz couldn't just marry Ruth outright. But would this other redeemer have the same compassion for Ruth that Boaz did? Perhaps not, but Boaz was a man of integrity and would do things the proper way and trust God with the results.

At the city gate, Boaz spoke with this relative about redeeming Naomi's property, as well as Ruth. Thankfully, this relative released his right to Boaz. Soon Boaz and Ruth were married, and before long, she had a son named Obed. Obed would go on to be the father of Jesse, the father of King David, part of the direct lineage of Jesus Christ. This concept of a family redeemer reminds us to love our neighbor as ourselves. Knowing Naomi and Ruth were destitute, Boaz showed great compassion and love through his generosity and kindness.

Pivot from the type of faith that loves only those who are able to love you back.

Pivot to the type of faith that doesn't look on temporary and typical human behavior as a litmus test on who to love but rather is able to know that everyone has a story, and everyone deserves to be loved.

Prayer
"Father, fill my heart with compassion and love for others. As people cross my path, give me Your love and insight into how to help them. In the name of Jesus, amen."

Your Pivotal Moment of Faith
Focus on kindness to others today and do something unexpected and helpful for a neighbor.

Job: Endurance and Faith in the Midst of Suffering

"Dear friends, do not be surprised at the fiery ordeal that has come on you to test you, as though something strange were happening to you. But rejoice inasmuch as you participate in the sufferings of Christ, so that you may be overjoyed when his glory is revealed." (1 Peter 4:12-13)

The story of Job gives a rare spiritual glimpse into the cosmic battle between God and Satan, the classic battle between good and evil. According to some scholars, Job is likely the oldest book in the Bible. At the beginning of the story, Satan is roaming across the earth and then appears before God in heaven. God says, "Look at my servant Job."

The Lord pointed to Job because he was different from other people. Living in the land of Nod, Job was prosperous with seven sons and daughters and a wealth of livestock and other animals. Satan told God, "Of course, Job loves You because he has everything going for him and is prosperous." So, God gave permission for Satan to take away Job's wealth. And that's exactly what Satan did. In a series of tragic events, all of Job's herds are stolen, and tragically, his children are killed. Yet, despite the heartbreak, Job was still able to say, "The LORD gave and the LORD has taken away; may the name of the LORD be praised" (Job 1:21).

But Satan didn't let up. Insisting that Job would curse God if he were to lose his health, God once again allowed the deceiver to strike. And so Satan afflicted Job with painful sores and boils.

In the chapters that follow four friends come to "comfort" Job in his misery. But their comfort amounted to little more than accusations—"only sinners deserve such suffering, so repent!" Even his own wife told Job to curse God and die.

Job endured heartbreak and suffering to a degree few people will ever experience. Yet throughout, his faith in God never wavered. And in the end, God restored to Job all that he had lost, and more (see Job 42:12).

The story of Job reminds us that God is able to orchestrate the details of our lives, even when the worst of the worst might happen. He does not always prevent or remove suffering from our life but instead uses these circumstances to teach us about God's character and His ultimate plan to shape our own character to benefit the Kingdom.

It's likely that through different periods of your life, you have endured sickness with a child or a parent. Perhaps your marriage has come apart through divorce and you have been fired from a position and then had to search for another job. Maybe you were driving on the freeway and were caught up in a multiple car accident. Throughout life, we face a number of these unexpected situations which cause suffering and pain. When life returns to normalcy, as it most often will, thinking about the circumstances and lessons can help you find your way through.

Pivot from the belief that you're somehow immune from trouble in this life.

Pivot to a relationship with God based on His character of love, His plan of redemption, and power for those of us who believe that He can influence our lives each day for the better.

Prayer
"Lord, I don't want to face trials and suffering but when I do, help me to understand You are orchestrating good to come out of the bad details of my life. Use my pain to grow my faith and deepen my relationship with You. In the name of Jesus, amen."

Your Pivotal Moment of Faith
Take a moment and reflect on some difficult situations from your own life or the life of a family member. How can your faith increase, and your gratitude and trust grow when you are in the middle of painful suffering? What can you learn from the example of Job?

Timothy: From Local Disciple to Trusted Ally

"All Scripture is God-breathed and is useful for teaching, rebuking, correcting and training in righteousness." (2 Timothy 3:16)

Sometimes painful experiences from the past provide new opportunities. In the book of Acts, the apostle Paul showed that he had much to learn. On his first missionary journey, Paul and Barnabas took along John Mark who bailed out of the trip and returned to Jerusalem. On his next trip Paul selected a young and eager Christian named Timothy as his assistant. Whatever challenges Timothy might have faced traveling with the apostle, Paul would eventually refer to Timothy as being like a son to him (see 1 Timothy 1:2).

Timothy was a native of Lystra and his mother Eunice and grandmother Lois were both Jews. These women brought Timothy up in the Christian faith and the Christians in his hometown highly respected him. When Paul and Barnabas first visited Lystra, Paul healed a man who had been crippled from birth and this miracle led many of the inhabitants to accept Paul's teaching. Now on his second missionary journey, Paul took Timothy. In his first letter to Timothy, Paul spoke prophetically about Timothy's special gifting of service. In order to not to offend the Jews in their travels, Paul had Timothy circumcised.

Through their travels, Timothy became one of Paul's most loyal and trusted assistants. Timothy was named as the co-author for 2 Corinthians, Philippians, Colossians, 1 Thessalonians, 2 Thessalonians, and Philemon. When Paul wrote to the Philippians about Timothy, he said, "I have no else one like him" (Philippians 2:20). It also seems Timothy had some physical ailment or illness. In his second letter to Timothy, Paul advised him to "Stop drinking only water, and use a little wine because of your stomach and your frequent illnesses" (1 Timothy 5:23). When Paul was in prison and awaiting martyrdom, he summoned his faithful friend Timothy for a last farewell.

Throughout his life, from all that we know, Timothy was a standout in the way he served Christ and his fellow believers. Often behind the scenes, Timothy was devoted to service to others and the work of the church. When it comes to leadership in the church, often Christians feel like they have to become a preacher or a teacher or a choir director of someone else with a visible role of leadership. Through the life and service of Timothy, we have a remarkable example of selfless devotion to God from which we can find the courage and consistency we need to serve God and others even from behind the scenes.

Pivot from believing that God mainly uses those with "up front" gifts.

Pivot to the truth that God uses any willing vessel who has set their heart to serve in any way to help others.

Prayer

"God, I celebrate and see the important ministry of service that Timothy shows us in the Scriptures. Show us how to find our gifting for the body whether in leadership or behind the scenes ministry. We trust You to guide the steps of our service. In the name of Jesus. Amen."

Your Pivotal Moment of Faith

Do you know your gifting? If so, write down a few of the gifts you believe God has given you to serve Him. If not, talk to trusted friends and mentors who know you well, and simply ask them what they feel your gifts might be. Their comments will likely identify your main giftings.

Thomas: Defeating Doubt

"Now faith is confidence in what we hope for and assurance about what we do not see."
(Hebrews 11:1)

Many people can easily express doubt and skepticism about various aspects of their faith, life, and work. One of Jesus' disciples expressed doubt at one point and has thus earned the nickname: Doubting Thomas.

The Scriptures do not tell us how Jesus called Thomas to become a disciple, and his name is only mentioned a few times. For example, in John 11, with the other disciples and Jesus, Thomas traveled to Bethany and saw Him talk with Mary and her sister, Martha. "If You had only been here, Lord, our brother Lazarus would still be alive." Thomas watched the painful scene and how it affected Jesus and could likely see the tears running down His cheeks. But that pain didn't linger because Jesus asked them to roll away the stone that closed the tomb.

Mary said, "Oh, Lord, we don't want to open this tomb because he has been in there four days and will begin to smell."

"Only have faith," Jesus said. So they rolled away the stone and Jesus commanded Lazarus to get up and come out of the tomb. Thomas was there with the other disciples to see Lazarus raised from the dead.

Fast forward to the days after Jesus' death. All of the disciples, except for Thomas, were gathered together when in their midst, the risen Lord appeared. When they later told Thomas about this miracle, he voiced doubt and skepticism.

"You must have imagined it," Thomas, who had witnessed the resurrection of Lazarus, said to his friends. "Unless I can touch His nail scarred hands and see the place in His side where the soldier pierced Him, I will not believe."

A week later, the disciples were gathered in an upper room with the door locked. In the middle of their group, Jesus appeared and said, "Peace be with you!" Then He looked straight at Thomas and said, "Touch the scars on my hands and then feel the wound in my side. Stop doubting and believe."

As Thomas touched the risen Lord Jesus, he worshipped saying, "My Lord and my God."

"Then Jesus told him, 'Because you have seen me, you have believed; blessed are those who have not see and yet have believed'" (John 20:29).

With the story of doubting Thomas, Jesus explains the essential nature of faith. We are called "blessed" because Christ followers today trust Jesus as our Lord and Savior as a step of faith and not through anything that we have seen with our eyes.

Pivot from allowing doubts to define you.

Pivot to allowing your doubts to drive you into finding out the truth of Jesus and His plan for your life.

Prayer
"Father, thank You for these stories about Thomas and how he saw Jesus and believed. Help my doubts and disbelief and lead me in faith to follow You. In Jesus' name. Amen."

Your Pivotal Moment of Faith
Write down a doubt or two that you've had, that you have now—by faith—turned into a firm belief. Now, write down a doubt or two you're still working through.

John: From Fisherman to Faithful Disciple

"Greater love has no one than this: to lay down one's life for one's friends." (John 15:13)

When Jesus of Nazareth began His three-year ministry, He walked along the sea of Galilee and called Peter and Andrew as the first two disciples to follow Him. Next Jesus called two more fishermen who were also brothers, named James and John. In a critical turning point in their lives, these two sons of Zebedee left their father and fishing nets to follow Jesus. Whenever these two men are mentioned in the Bible, John is always named after James and scholars assume John was younger than James.

Jesus gave these two brothers the nickname "Sons of Thunder" which may have indicated they were short-tempered and loud. John became a part of the inner circle of disciples. He was with Jesus when the Lord raised Jairus' daughter from the dead. He also joined Jesus on the mountain when He was transfigured, appearing with Moses and Elijah. Finally, during the last days of Jesus' life, John was one of the disciples invited to wait with Jesus in the Garden of Gethsemane. Jesus asked them to wait while He prayed a few feet away, and each time the disciples fell asleep.

At one point as John and James traveled with Jesus, these Sons of Thunder angered the other disciples with their special request to Jesus. They began their request with an unusual statement which did not leave room for any negotiation. "Teacher, we want You to do for us whatever we ask."

Listening Jesus asked, "What do you want me to do for you?"

With boldness they said, "When Your kingdom comes into fruition, let one of us sit on Your right and the other sit on Your left."

Jesus shook His head saying, "I don't believe you know what you are asking. Can you drink the cup I drink or be baptized with the baptism I am baptized with?"

In unison they replied, "We can."

"You both will follow my path, drink the cup that I drink and be baptized with the baptism that I am baptized with. But I cannot grant you to sit at my right or my left. These places belong to the people for whom they have been planned, and it is outside of anything I can control."

When the other ten disciples heard about the request from the brothers to Jesus, they became angry with James and John. To calm the dispute, Jesus made it a teachable moment. He called them together and said, "Our rulers and high officials exercise authority over others but that's not how you and I operate in the kingdom. If you want to be first, then you must be the slave of everyone else. Even the Son of Man did not come to be served but to serve others and give his life as a ransom for many."

Because John spent time with Jesus, he wrote one of the four Gospels to capture some of the stories about Jesus. John also wrote three letters to the churches 1-3 John and Revelation. His stories show a profound view of Jesus Christ and his letters to the churches gave moving inspiration about practical ways to live as Christians. John's stories about Jesus continue to help us today.

Pivot from any type of pride that makes you feel more special than others.

Pivot to the humility of a servant, both of Jesus and those in your network of relationships.

Prayer
"Lord, thank You for the faithful acts of obedience from John the disciple. Help me to grasp the depths of the humility of Jesus and then give me the humbleness of a servant. In the Holy Name of Jesus. Amen."

Your Pivotal Moment of Faith
Love of others was a constant theme of John the Disciple. Write down two or three reasons humility is needed to love others.

Joseph, Husband of Mary: Courageous Obedience

"'Does the LORD delight in burnt offerings and sacrifices as much as in obeying the LORD? To obey is better than sacrifice, and to heed is better than the fat of rams." (1 Samuel 15:22)

Often during the Christmas season each year, a key figure in the story is forgotten: a humble carpenter from Nazareth named Joseph. When he learned his fiancé Mary was pregnant, Joseph knew he was not the father of this child. Though in the Jewish culture an engagement was legally binding, Joseph knew he had to cancel his engagement and get a divorce. He didn't want to shame Mary publicly and planned to do it quietly. As Joseph faced this key point of decision, and was wondering what he should do, an angel of the Lord appeared to him in a dream. He heard him saying, "'Joseph, son of David, do not be afraid to take Mary home as your wife, because what is conceived in her is from the Holy Spirit. She will give birth to a son, and you are to give him the name Jesus, because he will save his people from their sins.' All this took place to fulfill what the Lord had said through the prophet: 'The virgin will conceive and give birth to a son, and they will call him Immanuel' (which means 'God with us')" (Matthew 1:20-23).

When Joseph woke up from the dream, he knew the entire situation was veiled in mystery but kept his marriage to Mary. But before the baby could be born, the Gospel of Luke says, Caesar Augustus decreed a census, and everyone had to return to their hometown to be counted. Joseph took Mary to Bethlehem, but all the rooms were full, so they stayed in a stable and the baby was born there. Joseph and Mary gave the child the name Jesus. Because Joseph was a direct descendant of King David, Jesus fulfilled the Old Testament prophecies as a "Son of David."

Shortly after Jesus was born, Joseph had another dream. In the dream the angel appeared to Joseph and warned him to flee to Egypt with Mary and the child to escape the wrath of Herod. That same night, Joseph, Mary and Jesus made the hard journey to Egypt where they stayed for several years. Joseph and his family stayed until they heard that Herod had died. With this news, they returned to Nazareth.

Throughout the early years of Jesus, Joseph certainly had questions about how the details were going to work out. Despite these questions, Joseph moved forward in obedience, to protect and save his family.

Much of the Christian life is understanding the life of faith is a journey in which we don't see the end but move forward each day in obedience as best we can. While Jesus will always understand and accept us as we are—even amidst our failings—obedience is for our benefit, not His.

Pivot from a self-reliant faith that only obeys when it's convenient.

Pivot to a God-reliant faith that understands obedience in the Christian life serves our own soul most of all.

Prayer
"Lord, thank You for how You directed the decisions and life of Joseph, the father of Jesus. Help us to learn to follow You in faith and obedience. Show us Your path for our days and lives. In the Name of Jesus. Amen."

Your Pivotal Moment of Faith
When have you taken a step of faith not knowing all of the details? How did God direct your steps?

Jephthah: From Rejected by Family to Leading Israel

"This is love: not that we loved God, but that he loved us and sent his Son as an atoning sacrifice for our sins." (1 John 4:10)

Do you recall as a kid how it felt when they divided up and picked teams in P.E.? It likely never happened but imagine yourself as the last person chosen for a team, and that feeling of being unwanted. It's what Jephthah had happen to him as a child. He was an unwanted brother. His father, Gilead, though married, he consorted with a prostitute and fathered Jephthah. At least Gilead acknowledged the boy Jephthah and took him into his home to raise. His brothers didn't accept this son from "another woman." When Gilead died and they were dividing his inheritance, the sons sent Jephthah away empty handed. They didn't realize they were rejecting a future judge of the nation of Israel. To escape the torment from his brothers, Jephthah fled to the land of Tob. In this new place, he settled and soon gathered a group of scoundrels around him who followed his leadership.

Sometime later, the Ammonites were fighting against Israel. The elders in Gilead (Gilead was both the name of Jephtha's father and country) went to get Jephthah in the land of Tob. "We need you to become our commander so we can fight the Ammonites for Israel."

Jephthah was confused to hear these words from the elders saying to them, "Didn't you hate me and drive me away from my father's house? Now that you are in trouble why do you come to me?"

The elders said, "We know it appears strange, but we need you to come lead us into battle against our enemy."

Skeptical, Jephthah said, "What if I go with you and lead you into battle and the Lord gives us success to win. Will you really have me as the leader of Gilead?"

"Before the Lord as our witness, we swear a solemn oath you will be our leader." Reassured, Jephthah went into battle. He threatened the King of the Ammonites, who ignored him and paid no attention. The Spirit of the Lord came on Jephthah and as Judges says: "Then Jephthah went over to fight the Ammonites, and the LORD gave them into his hands. He devastated twenty towns from Aroer to the vicinity of Minnith, as far as Abel Keramim. Thus, Israel subdued Ammon" (Judges 11:32-33).

Painful rejection, of course, would rarely be part of God's plan, but God proves time and time again that what others think is useless, God makes useful!

Pivot from any feelings of rejection from God. God has a purpose and plan for everyone. Sometimes it just takes some time to show the world what that is.

Pivot to the sheer truth of who you are in Christ. A unique creation with unique giftings to help others understand the Kingdom of God.

Prayer

"Lord, help me to understand in depth Your love for me each day and to pass that love on to others in my life. I want to learn the lesson of Jephthah; that I have purpose in life no matter my family background or odd choices. In Your name. Amen."

Your Pivotal Moment of Faith

Take a few moments to ponder your life up to this point. List three things you were put on earth for that no one else can do?

Joseph of Arimathea: From Secret Disciple to Displaying Reverence

"If I speak in the tongues of men or of angels, but do not have love, I am only a resounding gong or a clanging cymbal." (1 Corinthians 13:1)

Three of the four Gospels in the New Testament include the mention of Joseph of Arimathea. Arimathea was a village in the hill country of Ephraim, about twenty miles northwest of Jerusalem. Joseph was a member of the Sanhedrin who were a religious legislative body who decided the details of the law for all Israel. Politically, before the Romans took over Judea, this esteemed group of the Sanhedrin could appoint a king, the high priest, declare war, and expand the territory of Jerusalem and the Temple. In the era Jesus lived in, the Sanhedrin took care of any aspects of local government which were not in the hands of the Roman government. They tended to be wealthy and self-sufficient men who were focused on living in the present and not on the hereafter. They acted like wealth was the most important aspect of their lives and enjoyed the good life here and now. They were not concerned about whether you could take it with you or whether you needed to prepare for life beyond the grave.

During this period the religious community was constantly talking internally about the miracles of

Jesus and what to do about His teaching. Joseph of Arimathea listened to these conversations but didn't reveal he was a secret disciple of Jesus Christ. He watched the high priest Caiphas condemn Jesus and push the Roman governor Pilate to crucify Jesus before the start of Passover. In secret, Joseph watched the soldiers nail Jesus to a cross on Golgotha and then saw as He breathed His last and said, "It is finished."

While he didn't agree with the decision of the high priest, this secret follower of Jesus knew he must take action and do something about the broken body of the Savior. He knew he had to act quickly because Jesus had died on Preparation Day or the day before the Sabbath. He was thinking, "My tomb is a fitting burial place for Jesus Christ."

With a surge of boldness, Joseph went immediately to Pilate. He asked, "Will you please give me the body of Jesus? I have a new tomb and want to use it for his burial."

For Pilate, this request about Jesus was a surprise. "Has He already died?" Pilate summoned the centurion who quickly checked and learned that Jesus was dead. Pilate gave Joseph of Arimathea permission to take the body of Jesus. With care and attention, Joseph removed the body of Jesus from the cross, and he wrapped it with linen and carefully laid it in his new tomb. Finally, Joseph, likely with the help of Roman soldiers, rolled the stone to seal the tomb. Several women who had watched Jesus take His final breath followed Joseph from a distance and watched as he prepared the body and sealed the tomb.

This secret disciple teaches us a lesson in reverence. He revered Jesus so much he was willing to ruin his reputation. Joseph knew this was no ordinary man the Jews and Romans had killed. He was the Son of God and should be treated as such.

Pivot from seeing Jesus as just another religious name to hear about.

Pivot to putting Jesus in His proper place in our hearts in a way that show trues reverence for who He is, and who we are in comparison.

Prayer
"God, thank You for the boldness You gave this secret disciple of Jesus, Joseph of Arimathea and how his reverence for Jesus caused him to take action that could have cost him dearly with his peers. Give me that boldness to be a witness for You. In Your name. Amen."

Your Pivotal Moment of Faith
Does your faith in Jesus include a fair amount of reverence for who He is? Write down one way you can show your reverence for Jesus this week.

John Mark: Early Mistakes Don't Necessarily Define Your Future

"Bear with each other and forgive one another if any of you has a grievance against someone. Forgive as the Lord forgave you." (Colossians 3:13)

Some of the stories of the early days of the first Christians, after the resurrection of Jesus Christ, are captured in The Acts of the Apostles. Scripture tells us about the dramatic conversion of Paul on the road to Damascus and how Barnabas, the son of encouragement, befriended Paul and was one of his early instructors about the Way. Barnabas also traveled with Paul and on the first missionary journey he brought his young cousin, John Mark, along for the adventure. He wanted John Mark to travel with them to teach him how to share the Good News about Jesus with others. As they traveled to the various churches, John Mark traveled with them. He went to Cyprus and as far as Perga in Pamphylia when he decided to return to Jerusalem instead of continuing with Paul and Barnabas (Acts 13:13). While scholars have speculated about the reasons John Mark left, the Scriptures are silent about these details.

Paul and Barnabas completed their trips with the churches and returned to Jerusalem. As they prepared to make another trip, Barnabas suggested to Paul they give John Mark another opportunity to travel with them. Paul disagreed. An argument of some sort occurred, so Barnabas and John-Mark went one direction while Paul and Silas went in a different direction (Acts 15:36-40).

Barnabas was patient with his cousin John Mark. Then this young man repaid this investment with his work and renewed vigor for sharing the Good News during their travels. In a later trip, Paul reunited with John Mark and the older apostle became a close friend of this younger disciple.

John Mark spent a lot of time in Jerusalem and, in particular, with the Apostle Peter. Besides his travels mentioned in Acts, he also wrote the most straight-forward stories about Jesus in the Gospel of Mark.

Barnabas likely continued to play a key role in John Mark's life and kept up with his encouragement and teaching. Even when the apostle Paul refused to travel with John Mark, Barnabas stood by his cousin's side. This type of forbearance and support of others gives us an important example. Everyone deserves to be given a second and third opportunity when they miss the first one. When other Christians make mistakes, in general there are two ways to respond: decide not to interact with them any longer like Paul did at first or give them a second opportunity and provide encouragement as Barnabas did.

Pivot from believing that you—or others—are beyond redemption.

Pivot to knowing that no one—including you—should be judged based on his or her worst actions on any given day. Instead, when someone is ready to step up and renew their courage as one of Jesus' disciples, they should be given another chance.

Prayer

"Father, when others make mistakes, help me to forgive them and encourage them with another opportunity like Barnabas did for Mark. Open doors for me to encourage others. In Jesus' name."

Your Pivotal Moment of Faith

There is likely at least one person in your life who needs someone to support them, despite their past. Take the time to contact that friend and offer the love and support they need.

Barnabas: The Encourager

"If it is to encourage, then give encouragement; if it is giving, then give generously; if it is to lead, do it diligently; if it is to show mercy, do it cheerfully."
(Romans 12:8)

Early in the pages of the Acts of the Apostles, Luke introduces Joseph, who has a nickname of Barnabas or "son of Encouragement." To provide practical encouragement, Barnabas sold a field and brought those funds to the Apostles so it could be distributed to anyone in need (Acts 4:36-37). This simple action from Barnabas of selling his field and giving all of the funds to the church stood in sharp contrast to two other early disciples, Ananias and Sapphira.

This couple also sold a property. But when Ananias presented the money to Peter, he claimed it was the full amount that he had received for selling the land. Peter discerned the truth right away and knew that Ananias was lying; he had kept some of the money back for himself. Ananias dropped dead on the spot. And when Sapphira, his wife, came by later and was asked the same question, she told the same lie, and met the same fate. Their sin wasn't in keeping money back for themselves, instead it was in lying about what they gave to make their contribution seem more generous than it was. Rather than being an encouragement to the early church, like Barnabas, these two served as a warning and tragic example.

Barnabas was one of the leaders and teachers in the early church. He knew of the Pharisee named Saul who had gotten letters from the chief priests against the believers in Damascus. On the way to Damascus, Saul had a vision of Jesus Christ which left him blinded until he met a disciple Ananias who baptized Saul and helped him escape from the city.

When Saul—now renamed Paul—returned to Jerusalem, the majority of the Christians were terrified and hesitant to welcome Paul into their midst. Wasn't he the man who hated and wanted to kill Christians? But this son of encouragement, Barnabas, disregarded the church's fear and welcomed Paul into the circle of believers (Acts 9:27). As Barnabas spent time with Paul, he even traveled with him on his first missionary journey to the various cities in Asia. Before long, the church at Antioch sent Paul and Barnabas out as missionaries to other cities in the region. In many ways this encourager was an influential leader in the early church, and he taught the believers that true obedience to God will often involve risk.

When someone crosses our path who is an easy target for criticism, we should catch ourselves from doing so when others seem to want to pile on. Life can be hard, and we are all prone to making mistakes. Instead of bending toward criticism, bend toward encouragement. As believers we hold the power to build someone up. Let's be a builder.

Pivot from the natural tendency to offer criticism to someone when they fail to meet expectations.

Pivot to your first response being one of encouragement to help them be their better selves.

Prayer

"God, thank You for the practical lessons of encouragement from the life of Barnabas. Help me to take risks and encourage others in their faith journey. In Your name. Amen."

Your Pivotal Moment of Faith

One person in your life needs some encouragement. It may even be you. Figure out the person and figure out how to best give them courage.

Abigail: Peaceful Resolution of Conflict

"If it is possible, as far as it depends on you, live at peace with everyone." (Romans 12:18)

Saul, the first king of Israel was proving to be a problem. Because of his disobedience, the Lord turned had away from him. And so God had sent Samuel, the last judge and first prophet in Israel to anoint David, a young shepherd to be the next king. When Saul heard about this, he became jealous and sought to kill David. But David, with his own supporters, fled. Constantly on the move, David and his men, on one occasion, had protected the sheep of a wealthy man near Carmel named Nabal, whose name meant "fool." Nabal had a reputation for being a cruel, selfish, and mean man.

David asked Nabal to share provisions for his men as a gesture of gratitude for the protection David's men had provided Nabal and his flocks. Instead of a gracious response, Nabal said to David's servants, "Who is this man named David? Who is this son of Jesse? These days many servants are breaking away from their masters. Why should I take my bread, water, and meat which I have slaughtered for my shearers, and give it to these outlaws?" (See 1 Samuel 25:10-11)

This response from Nabal offended David and when he heard the response, he commanded his men to take up their swords. About 400 men responded.

Meanwhile, one of Nabal's servants went to Nabal's wife, Abigail. This servant explained, "David's men have been very good to us and have stolen nothing from us whenever they have been with us. In fact, it was like they provided a wall of protection around us and the sheep. But when David asked for supplied, Nabal hurled insults back at him. You need to figure out how to calm down this conflict or there is going to be trouble for Nabal and his whole family."

Abigail quickly launched into action. She gathered 200 loaves of bread and two skins of wine. She had five sheep slaughtered and prepared them to eat. Then she gathered five bushels of roasted grain, 100 cakes of raisins, 200 cakes of pressed figs and had the servants load everything on donkeys. "Go to David and I will follow you," Abigail told them, but said nothing to her husband, Nabal.

As she rode down the mountain with her donkey, David and his men were on their up, ready to lay waste to Nabal and his land.

Abigail pleaded with David to forgive the disrespectful response from her husband, Nabal. David graciously forgave Nabal's offence and told her to go home in peace. Shortly after she returned home, the Lord struck Nabal, and he died about ten days later. Nabal and Abigail had two different approaches to handling conflict. While Nabal used insults, Abigail responded with generosity and compassion. What lessons can we learn when conflict comes into our life?

Pivot from harboring unforgiveness in any form in your heart. It dishonors what God has done for you and keeps you from having any ministry in the lives of others.

Pivot to understanding the gravity of your own sin in the eyes of God—and His response to you of total forgiveness; a gift we always need to give to others.

Prayer
"Father, when there is conflict, help me to have understanding and use the lessons of generosity and compassion from Abigail instead of acting with the impulsive insults of Nabal. In the name of Jesus. Amen."

Your Pivotal Moment of Faith
When you have a conflict with someone do you have an impulse to listen and resolve with respect or respond with an insult?

Silas: A Selected Co-minister for Paul

"God is our refuge and strength, an ever-present help in trouble. Therefore, we will not fear, though the earth give way and the mountains fall into the heart of the sea." (Psalm 46:1-2)

The Book of Acts shows the expansion of the early church from Jerusalem to other cities. Paul, the apostle, was visiting churches and for his second missionary journey selected a leader in the Jerusalem church named Silas as a companion. While in the city of Troas (in what is now Turkey), during the night, Paul had a vision where he saw a Macedonian man begging him to come to Macedonia and help them. After this vision, Paul and Silas immediately left for Macedonia to preach the Gospel to them. They reached Philippi, which was a Roman colony and the leading city in the district of Macedonia.

Paul and Silas were headed to their regular place of prayer and were face to face with a female slave who had an evil spirit which allowed her to predict the future. For her owners, this slave earned a lot of money through her predictions of the future. For many days, this slave followed Silas and Paul. She continually shouted, "These men are servants of the Most High God and are telling you the way to be saved." Day after day this woman continued to follow, annoy, and shout around Silas and Paul.

One day, Paul turned to the woman and said to the spirit, "In the name of Jesus Christ, I command you to come out of her." At that moment the spirit left, and her owners could see their money-making business had suddenly disappeared. The owners seized the men and dragged them to the authorities demanding Paul and Silas be arrested and jailed. The crowd jeered in agreement and the magistrates arrested Silas and Paul, then had them beaten and thrown into prison. These leaders ordered the jailer to carefully watch these men, and he threw the pair into an inner cell and fastened their feet in stocks.

While it was a strange place to sing, about midnight Silas and Paul were praying in the prison and singing hymns with the other prisoners listening. A violent earthquake shook the prison, and it opened the doors, and everyone's chains fell off. Awake from the earthquake, the jailer saw the open doors and assumed everyone had escaped, so he took his sword intending to kill himself. Paul stopped him saying, "Don't kill yourself. Everyone is here."

The jailer called for lights, and then rushed to Paul and Silas asking, "What must I do to be saved?"

"'Believe in the Lord Jesus and you will be saved—you and your household'" (Acts 16:31). At that hour, the jailer washed their wounds and he and all his household were baptized. That next morning the magistrates sent word to release Paul and Silas. But Paul asked, "Was it lawful for them to arrest two Roman citizens without a trial? We are Roman citizens and need your apology and an escort out of the city." After securing both, Paul and Silas left the city.

Being in a supportive role, Silas was exactly what Paul needed in a ministry partner. Though he was a leader in the Jerusalem church, Silas took on more of a supportive role when he was traveling with Paul. Some people are called to be the upfront leader, but most of us serve God in the background.

Pivot from the possible need to be upfront in your ministry unless God has made it evident for you to do so.

Pivot to being comfortable and fulfilled as a joyful behind-the-scenes minister.

Prayer
"God, thank You that You have created each of us for different tasks at different times. Help me realize the place You have for me and to be content in any position that moves Your Kingdom forward. In Your name. Amen."

Your Pivotal Moment of Faith
What lessons might you think Silas learned by being Paul's partner in ministry?

Lydia: An Untrained Believer Moves Forward

"Be on your guard; stand firm in the faith; be courageous; be strong. Do everything in love."
(1 Corinthians 16:13-14)

The Book of Acts documents the exciting story of how the Good News about Jesus spread from the Jews in Jerusalem to the Gentiles throughout the known world. In Acts 16, the Scriptures introduce a successful businesswoman from Thyatira named Lydia. While a Gentile, Lydia accepted the basic Jewish teachings about the one true God and attended Jewish services.

Lydia sold the purple cloth used to create beautifully designed clothing for important and royal Romans. While visiting Philippi on business, Lydia went to nearby river and celebrated God's Holy Day with other worshipers. Instead of a building, they met at the riverbank for prayer which gave them a quiet and peaceful place for their worship.

During this particular day God brought the Apostle Paul to this same riverbank where Lydia was gathered with other women celebrating the sabbath. As Paul preached the Gospel message about Jesus Christ, Lydia listened attentively to the preaching of the Word of God. After hearing the Scriptures, Lydia opened her heart and embraced the saving grace of Jesus Christ. She then publicly confessed her faith (Acts 16:14).

Almost immediately doors opened for Lydia to share her newfound faith with others and bring them to faith in Christ. As a result of Lydia's testimony, her entire household trusted Christ as Savior. As a public sign of their commitment to Jesus Christ, the members of Lydia's household were baptized. Lydia had a gift of hospitality as remarkable as her faith. "'If you consider me a believer in the Lord,' she said, 'come and stay at my house'" (Acts 16:15). Paul and his companions went to Lydia's home which became a gathering place for the Christians.

Lydia is now regarded as the first European convert to Christianity. Her gracious acts of hospitality paved the way for the ministry of the church to spread beyond its Judean origins. This work of God began in Lydia's heart and then He used her to spread the Good News about Jesus to many others.

What opportunities or challenges is God placing in front of you? Is He moving in your heart to share the Gospel of Jesus? Maybe God is asking you to do something courageous in your workplace. He may guide you to tell the story of Jesus with your family or speak at your church of the hope of Jesus. It took courage for Lydia to embrace God's work in her heart and life. How will God use the courage of Lydia in your own relationship with Jesus?

Pivot from believing that God can't really use you because you're not educated or trained.

Pivot to knowing that God can use anyone with a willing heart to help others along their faith journey.

Prayer

"Father, thank You for how You used the courage and faith of Lydia and brought her to a place where her heart to serve overcame any reluctance or doubt that she was ready to do so. Help me to learn from her example and use my life to bring others to faith in Jesus. In His name, amen."

Your Pivotal Moment of Faith

What does courage look like to you? Think of one way you could have more courage as you seek to live your faith.

Mary, Mother of Jesus: Simple Faith

"'My soul glorifies the Lord and my spirit rejoices in God my Savior.'" (Luke 1:46-47)

The experience would shock anyone. Mary, a teenager, was engaged to be married to Joseph, the carpenter in Nazareth. Unexpectedly the angel Gabriel appeared to her and said, "'Greetings, you who are highly favored! The Lord is with you'" (Luke 1:28). The Bible describes Mary as "troubled" as she wondered about the meaning of such a greeting. Gabriel continued to tell her that she would bear a son who was to be named Jesus. This son would sit on the throne of King David and His reign would never end. Naturally, as a virgin, Mary wondered how such a thing could happen.

"The angel answered, 'The Holy Spirit will come on you, and the power of the Most High will overshadow you. So the holy one to be born will be called the Son of God'" (Luke 1:35).

Instead of running or doubting or protesting, Mary did neither of these actions. Instead, she turned and responded to the call of God with humility and faith. "'I am the Lord's servant,' Mary answered. 'May your word to me be fulfilled'" (Luke 1:38). And then Mary prayed a beautiful prayer:

"'My soul glorifies the Lord, and my spirit rejoices in God my Savior, for he has been mindful of the humble state of his servant. From now on all generations will call me blessed, for the Mighty One has done great things for me—holy is his name. His mercy extends to those who fear him, from generation to generation. He has performed mighty deeds with his arm; he has scattered those who are proud in their inmost thoughts. He has brought down rulers from their thrones but has lifted up the humble. He has filled the hungry with good things but has sent the rich away empty. He has helped his servant Israel, remembering to be merciful to Abraham and his descendants forever, just as he promised our ancestors" (Luke 1:46-55).

As a virgin, Mary faced the pressure and judgement of society when she made this pivotal response. The angel's news transformed her ordinary life. She would become the mother of Jesus, the Son of God and Savoir of the world.

Throughout the centuries, Mary, the mother of Jesus, has become a model of simple obedience and faithful action to her calling. As you read the stories like this one in the Bible, God will use them to direct your steps but only if you are listening and committed to taking action. The first step in the process is to be sensitive to God's direction and His Spirit as you read the Scriptures. More than listening, you also need to take action as God directs your steps.

Pivot from trying to overthink your role in the Kingdom.

Pivot to an uncomplicated belief that God knows what He's doing as it relates to your life and then be ready to fulfill any call God would place in your path.

Prayer

"Lord, thank You for the example of Mary and her simple faith and trust in Your guidance in her life. Help me to learn from her example in my own life. In Your name. Amen."

Your Pivotal Moment of Faith

God can only direct our steps if we are listening to His Spirit through a consistent reading of Scripture and contemplative prayer. What practical steps can you take to be ready to follow God's voice as He directs your path?

Ananias of Damascus: Fearful Yet Obedient

"When I am afraid, I put my trust in you."
(Psalm 56:3)

During the early days of the church, the Jewish religious leaders were attacking Christians. When Stephen was arrested for his faith, then taken to be stoned to death, a Pharisee named Saul, was present. Many of the Christians feared Saul because he was known for his zeal in hunting down believers of the Messiah. In fact, the leaders of the Pharisees gave Saul approval to extend his search to Damascus. While on the road to Damascus a flash of light appeared from heaven around Saul. Saul fell to the ground and heard a voice say, "Saul, Saul why do you persecute me?"

"'Who are you, Lord?' Saul asked.

"'I am Jesus, whom you are persecuting,' he replied. 'Now get up and go into the city, and you will be told what you must do'" (Acts 9:4-6). When Saul opened his eyes, he was blind, and his companions had to lead him into the city. Saul was blind for three days and didn't eat or drink anything.

Inside the city of Damascus, Ananias, a disciple of Jesus, was praying and in a vision, the Lord spoke his name, "Ananias."

Jesus spoke with him saying, "Get up and go to the road called Straight to the house of Judas. When there, ask for Saul of Tarsus who is praying. In a vision, he has seen that Ananias is coming to him so you can touch him and restore his sight."

Ananias objected, "But Lord, I've heard about this man and how he has hurt and harmed believers in Jerusalem. The chief priests have given him authority to arrest anyone who calls on your name."

Jesus continued, "Go to him. This man is my chosen vessel to proclaim my name to the Gentile people, Kings and to the people of Israel. I will show him how much he must suffer for my name."

Immediately Ananias went to the house of Judas and saw Saul. "Brother Saul, Jesus sent me to you so you can see again and be filled with the Holy Spirit." As Ananias touched Saul, scales fell from the blind man's eyes and his sight was restored. Saul was baptized and then ate to restore his strength. For several days he stayed with the Damascus believers.

Ananias played an important part in the first days of the early church. Putting aside his fears, he trusted God and witnessed the transformation that took place in the heart of the greatest enemy of the Christians at the time. Though at first, Ananias argued with the Lord's direction, he understood that God directs our steps—even we can't see the end of the journey. From Ananias we must learn the courage of following God's voice, believing in people, and trusting God in the lives of others.

Pivot from having any fear in sharing your story with anyone in your sphere of relationships.

Pivot to having the courage of Ananias to speak truth in a kind way to those you love.

Prayer
"God thank You for how You directed the steps of Ananias and gave him the courage to follow Your will. Give me the faith to follow the direction of the Holy Spirit in my day. In the name of Jesus Amen."

Your Pivotal Moment of Faith
Is there one person you've debated sharing your faith with that is "difficult?" Write down their name and take some time to pray for them and then pray for an opportunity to share your story.

Balaam: When A Donkey Spoke

"'For I know the plans I have for you,' declares the LORD, 'plans to prosper you and not to harm you, plans to give you hope and a future.'"
(Jeremiah 29:11)

After leaving Egypt, the Hebrew people wandered in the wilderness for 40 years as punishment. But as the time drew near for them to finally claim the land God promised, the Israelites began conquering many of the neighboring nations. When King Balak of the Moabites saw how easily the Jewish people had conquered the Amorites, the king had to do something to protect his people in Moab.

The king sent messengers to Balaam, a well-known diviner, who lived in his area and said, "Come to me and put a curse on these people because I know whoever you curse is cursed and whoever you bless is blessed."

That night, God spoke to Balaam in a dream and asked, "Who are these men who have come to you?"

Balaam answered the Lord, "The King of Moab, Balak son of Zippor sent me a message that a people had come out of Egypt and covered the land. Now they want me to put a curse for them and maybe it will drive them away."

God warned Balaam, "Do not go with these people. You must not curse the people who have come out of Egypt because they are blessed."

When Balaam got up the next morning, he went to Balak's men and said, "Go back home to your king. I will not be going with you because the Lord will not let me."

The Moabite officials went back to King Balak and said, "Balaam refused to come with us." The king did not accept Balaam's refusal. He sent more distinguished men to Balaam saying, "You will receive a great fee from me if you will curse these people for me." After multiple refusals, Balaam answered them saying, "Even if King Balak gave me all of the gold and silver in his palace, I could not do anything outside of God's command. Spend the night here and I will find out what else the Lord tells me."

God appeared to Balaam and said, "You may go with these men, but you can only tell them whatever I say to you." Balaam changed directions because the Lord gave him permission. The next morning, Balaam saddled his donkey and went with the Moabite officials. God was angry with Balaam and sent an angel to stand in the road. When the donkey saw the angel, he veered out of the road and Balaam beat his animal. Three times Balaam tried to move the donkey forward but each time he disobeyed and was beaten. Finally, the Lord made the donkey speak and he said, "What have I done that you beat me three time?"

Balaam said, "You made me look like a fool. If I had a sword, I would kill you."

The donkey said, "I'm your donkey which you have always ridden. Have I ever done anything like this before?"

"No," Balaam said. Then the Lord opened Balaam's eyes and he saw the angel standing in the road with a drawn sword. He understood why his donkey had avoided the road.

The Lord said, "If your donkey had not swerved, I would have killed you and spared the donkey. You may go with these men but only speak what I tell you to speak."

Balaam followed the Lord and despite what King Balak wanted, he never cursed the Jewish people.

Pivot from the belief that God is not able to tell you what to speak to others.

Pivot to the firm knowledge that God is living and active and able to guide you as you share the Kingdom message to your friends and family.

Prayer
"God, thank You that You can use a simple talking donkey to direct Balaam. Give me listening ears as I read the Bible to guide and direct my life. Amen."

Your Pivotal Moment of Faith
List one way the Lord guides your life through His Word. How does He show you His will?

Jehoshaphat: An Unexpected Way to Win the Battle

"'Do not be afraid or discouraged because of this vast army. For the battle is not yours, but God's.'"
(2 Chronicles 20:15)

Throughout the Old Testament battles were fought hand to hand with swords. But as Israel discovered on more than one occasion, when God is fighting for you, anything can happen. One such battle happened during the reign of King Jehoshaphat.

During this period, the Moabites, Ammonites, and the Meunites waged war against Jehoshaphat.

Some people came to the king and said, "There is a great army coming against you."

Alarmed at this news, Jehoshaphat decided to ask the Lord what to do and first proclaimed a fast for everyone in Judah. People from all over Judah gathered in Jerusalem at the temple of the Lord and said, "'LORD, the God of our ancestors, are you not the god who is in heaven? ... Power and might are in your hand, and no one can withstand you. ... We have no power to face this vast army that is attacking us. We do not know what to do, but our eyes are on you'" (2 Chronicles 20:6,12).

As the people assembled, the Spirit of the Lord came on Jahaziel, a Levite. "He said: 'Listen, King Jehoshaphat and all who live in Judah and Jerusalem! This is what the LORD says, "Do not be afraid or discouraged because of this vast army. For the battle is not yours, but God's... You will not have to fight this battle. Take up your positions; stand firm and see the deliverance the LORD will give you, Judah and Jerusalem"'" (2 Chronicles 20:15,17).

With this prophetic word from the Lord, Jehoshaphat bowed down with his face to the ground, and all the people of Judah and Jerusalem fell down in worship before the Lord.

Early in the morning they left for the Desert of Tekoa. After consulting the people, Jehoshaphat appointed men to sing as they went out at the head of the army, saying, "Give thanks to the Lord, for his love endures forever."

As the people sang praise, they climbed toward the battlefield. As they moved forward toward their enemy, the Lord set ambushes against the men of Ammon and Moab and Mount Seir and they were defeated.

As the army of Israel came to a place that overlooked the desert, they saw only the dead bodies of their enemies lying on the ground; no one had escaped. Jehoshaphat and his men went to carry off their plunder, and they found so much that it took three days to collect it. Then King Jehoshaphat led all the men of Judah and Jerusalem to return joyfully to Jerusalem, for the Lord had given them cause to rejoice over their enemies. They entered Jerusalem and went to the temple of the Lord with harps and lyres and trumpets. The fear of God came on all the surrounding kingdoms when they heard how the Lord had fought against the enemies of Israel. And the kingdom of Jehoshaphat was at peace, for his God had given him rest on every side. Instead of a physical fight, Israel trusted in the Lord, and God took care of the battle.

When you have a challenge or problem, how can you focus on praising and worshiping God, and leaving your concerns in His hands?

Pivot from fighting your battles using your own strength.

Pivot to praising God for the answer that He will give you as you seek to become a more courageous disciple willing to fight for the faith of others.

Prayer
"Lord, thank You for this example from King Jehoshaphat about how You went ahead of Your people to fight their battle. Help me to spend more time in praise and worship rather than doubt and fear. In Jesus' name. Amen."

Your Pivotal Moment of Faith
Do you have a battle you're facing that could use a dose of praise and surrender to allow God the chance to go before you? Name it here and track with God how He will help win the battle for His glory.

Bartimaeus: Persistent Cries for Jesus' Attention

"You need to persevere so that when you have done the will of God, you will receive what he has promised." (Hebrews 10:36)

For three years, Jesus of Nazareth ministered to the Jewish people in Israel. As He taught the crowds, He also healed many of them from diseases and demons. On two different occasions, Jesus fed thousands of people. Also, Jesus had raised several people from the dead. The news of these amazing miracles spread like wildfire through the region.

Mark chapter 10 tells of a time when a blind man had to try a little harder to get the attention of the Healer. One day Jesus and His disciples came into Jericho, which was eighteen miles northeast of Jerusalem. They were leaving the city with a large crowd following closely behind. These people were animated and excited. Some of them were shouting. Children likely joined them, skipping along. The snippets of conversations were about Jesus, the Son of the Living God. He had decided to pass right along the street through Jericho. Various songs of praise could be heard from the crowd following Him.

Listening to all this commotion was a blind man named Bartimaeus who made his living by begging. When he heard from the crowd that Jesus of Nazareth was passing by, he began to shout, "Jesus, Son of David, have mercy on me!"

As Bartimaeus shouted and made noise, various people in the crowd told him to "Be quiet" and tried to stop his shouting.

"Blind man, don't bother, Jesus," they said.

Bartimaeus knew his opportunity to speak with Jesus was going to disappear. The rebukes and cautions from the crowd only stirred Bartimaeus into a greater frenzy saying, "Son of David, have mercy on me!"

Through the crowd, Jesus heard the cries of Bartimaeus. He stopped and said, "Call him."

The crowd changed their reaction and called to Bartimaeus saying, "Cheer up! On your feet! He's calling you."

Bartimaeus threw off his cloak and jumped up as Jesus came near. With a look of compassion, Jesus looked at the blind man and asked, "What do you want me to do for you?"

Bartimaeus said, "Rabbi, I want to see."

With a nod of agreement, Jesus smiled and said, "Go. Your faith has healed you." Bartimaeus instantly received his sight and followed Jesus along the road. The crowd celebrated this well-known beggar who was blind but could now see.

This story shows the loving care of the Lord Jesus for a man who was in desperate straits to see Him. Just ten days later, Jesus would be arrested and crucified. The Gospel of Mark captured this simple story when Jesus took a moment with a blind beggar and gave him sight.

As we pray and ask the Lord for a miracle or a change in our own lives, we can learn from the persistence of Bartimaeus.

Pivot from being a passive follower of Jesus.

Pivot to becoming a bit more thankful, a bit more daring, and a bit more dependent follower of Jesus.

Prayer
"God, we never know how You are going to answer our prayers—yes, no, or wait. Help me to have the courage and persistence of a Bartimaeus as I seek Your will for my life. In the name of Jesus. Amen."

Your Pivotal Moment of Faith
What lessons about simple faith, persistence and seizing the opportunity do you learn from the life of Bartimaeus?

Esau: Reconciliation

"Restore to me the joy of your salvation and grant me a willing spirit, to sustain me." (Psalm 51:12)

After Jacob spent years working in the land of Haran for his father-in-law Laban, he decided to go back to his homeland with his family and his livestock. The Lord told Jacob to return to the land of his fathers and that He would be with him. Without telling Laban, Jacob and his family and animals left for Canaan.

Throughout the journey, Jacob was understandably worried about how his brother Esau would receive them in Canaan. Many years earlier, Jacob had stolen Esau's birthright and blessing. And as Jacob made his escape, Esau promised to kill his brother. So as a peace offering to his brother, Jacob sent messengers ahead to meet his brother Esau to say he was coming with his family and animals. The messengers returned saying, "Esau is coming to meet you along with 400 men."

The news struck Jacob with fear, and he divided his family and animals into two groups. He also sent a servant with another gift for Esau of 200 female goats and 20 male goats, 200 ewes and 20 rams, 30 female camels with their young, 40 cows and 10 bulls, and 20 female donkeys and 10 male donkeys.

When Esau saw the extravagant gift he asked, "Who owns these animals and where are you going?"

The servant answered, "These animals belong to your servant Jacob. These are a gift sent to my lord Esau, and Jacob is coming behind us." Then a second group and third group of animals came with the same message to Esau. Jacob sent these animals as a gift to pacify his brother and prepare for their meeting.

The next morning, Jacob looked up and could see Esau coming toward him with his 400 men. He arranged his female servants and their children, then Leah and her children and finally Rachel and Joseph in the rear. The moment had finally come. Jacob greeted his brother and bowed down to the ground seven times. "But Esau ran to meet Jacob and embraced him; he threw his arms around his neck and kissed him. And they wept" (Genesis 33:4). Rather than greeting his brother with a knife, Esau accepted Jacob with open arms. And though he tried to refuse the extravagant gifts Jacob had sent ahead, Jacob insisted.

We don't really know what happened to Esau in the 20 years that Jacob was away. But by his reaction, we can see that Esau truly missed his brother.

Heartaches and heartbreaks caused by family members are some of the deepest hurts we'll ever feel. But lots of things can happen to a person over twenty years. And whether you wronged someone in the past, or someone wronged you, reconciliation may still be possible.

Pivot from letting a past mistake or pride keep you from reconciling with someone you know.

Pivot to being an initiator with those in your life with whom you need to reconcile.

Prayer
"Father, thank You for the restoration and forgiveness example You gave us with Jacob and Esau. Help me to be quick to forgive and reconcile with others. In the name of Jesus, amen."

Your Pivotal Moment of Faith
Recall a time when you have wronged someone else and then asked for and received forgiveness. Is there anyone else in your life that God is asking you to reconcile with?

Queen of Sheba: A Seeker of Truth

*"For the LORD gives wisdom; from his mouth
comes knowledge and understanding."
(Proverbs 2:6)*

During the reign of Solomon as King of Israel, his wisdom and insight spread throughout the known world. Many people retold the story that is now recorded for us in 1 Kings 3. Two woman had each given birth to a son. Sadly, one of the babies had died and the two women fought over the living baby, each claiming it as their own. They came to Solomon for him to determine which woman was the mother.

'Bring me a sword and we will kill the child," Solomon declared.

One of the women agreed with the ruling.

But the second mother responded differently saying, "No, don't kill the child. Let the other woman have the living child."

Solomon wisely discerned that the true mother of the child would rather see him live in another home than to see him die. So he ordered that the baby be given to the mother who asked for mercy because. This story was one of countless stories told of the unusual wisdom and insight of King Solomon.

Across the Arabian desert, the Queen of Sheba heard the stories about the wisdom of King Solomon. She was skeptical about them and said to herself, "They must be exaggerations of this king. I must see it for myself."

Gathering a large group of attendants, they loaded gifts of spices, gold and precious jewels on a caravan of camels then traveled hundreds of miles across until they arrived in Jerusalem.

When the Queen of Sheba met with King Solomon, she asked him many questions about various topics. To her amazement, King Solomon answered every question in a thorough way which satisfied her. As the queen spent time with King Solomon, she was surprised to see the reports about Solomon regarding his achievements and his wisdom were true. As she examined the details of the food on his table, how he ordered the seating of his officials, the robes of his servant and even the burnt offerings he made at the Lord's temple, she was overwhelmed.

The Queen of Sheba said, "The report I heard in my own country about your achievements and your wisdom is true. But I did not believe these things until I came and saw with my own eyes. Indeed, not even half was told me; in wisdom and wealth you have far exceeded the report I heard. How happy your people must be! How happy your officials who continually stand before you and hear your wisdom! Praise be to the LORD your God, who has delighted in you and placed you on the throne of Israel'" (1 Kings 10:6-9)."

While the Queen of Sheba came to Jerusalem as a skeptic, her attitude, mind and heart changed because of what she witnessed in the court of King Solomon. The Queen of Sheba was a seeker of truth and even Jesus commended her search for truth (Matthew 12:42). The Queen of Sheba can teach us how to handle the skeptics who come into our lives hoping to find truth.

Pivot from believing the skeptics are beyond reach.

Pivot to knowing that God's truth can eventually soften even the hardest hearts and move them closer to a genuine relationship with God.

Prayer
"God, thank You for how You changed the Queen of Sheba from a skeptic to a believer through the wisdom of King Solomon. Use the Scriptures in my life to guide me to the truth and help others come to know You. In Your Name. Amen."

Your Pivotal Moment of Faith
What story from your own life can you tell a skeptical friend that will encourage them to read the Bible and soak in the truth of God's Word?

The Widow of Zarephath: Giving All She Could

"A generous person will prosper; whoever refreshes others will be refreshed." (Proverbs 11:25)

On the edge of the village of Zarephath, a widow was gathering sticks to make a fire in her home. Famine had come to this land and this widow knew when she mixed her flour and oil today, it would be the last of the food for her and her son.

As she turned toward her home, a stranger, Elijah the prophet, approached her and asked, "Can you give me a drink of water?"

"Yes," she said, "Come inside and I will give you the water."

Elijah said, "And if it is not too much trouble, please give me a piece of bread too."

The widow shook her head and explained, "I can't help you because this small amount of flour and oil are all I have left for myself and my son so we can eat and then die."

Elijah said to her, "Don't be afraid. I come to you in the name of the Lord God of Israel. Use your oil and flour to make me some bread, then continue pouring and make more bread for you and your son."

The widow changed direction and made the bread as the prophet asked. Then she started cooking with more flour and oil for her son. The prophet told her, "You will have oil and flour from the Lord God until the rains return."

As the prophet said, the oil and the flour continued to pour out for the widow every day to feed Elijah and the widow and her son.

Later, the son of the widow became gravely ill, and his breathing grew more shallow until it stopped and he died. The widow sent word to the prophet Elijah, "What do you have against me, Elijah?" Did you come to remind me of my sin and kill my son?"

The prophet came to the widow's home and carried the body of the son upstairs to a room she had prepared for the prophet. Elijah put the son on his bed, then stretched his body on the son's body praying, "'LORD my God, let this boy's life return to him!'" (1 Kings 17:21).

As Elijah prayed, and the life returned to the son. Elijah carried the son back to the arms of his mother and she exclaimed, "Now I know that you are a man of God and speak truth from God." The simple trust and faith of widow of Zarephath moved her from hopelessness and despair to joy and faith in the God of Israel.

Pivot from believing there is a finite supply to meet the needs of others.

Pivot to knowing that with God, nothing is impossible, and there are infinite ways God can meet a need in the hour of trouble. He's a God who shows up.

Prayer

"God, some days are challenging. I celebrate how You used Elijah with the widow of Zarephath to change her situation. Help me to see challenges as opportunities to trust You and increase my faith. In Your name, amen."

Your Pivotal Moment of Faith

Is there a need in your life that God needs to "show up" for? Don't be timid about asking for His help, even if the odds don't seem in your favor. With God, all things are possible!

Huldah: Boldly Speaking God's Truth

"The wicked flee though no one pursues, but the righteous are as bold as a lion." (Proverbs 28:1)

During the days of King Josiah in Judah, Huldah was a prophet of the Lord and courageously proclaimed God's truth to the people in Judah. King Josiah was twenty-six and had ordered Hilkiah and the other priests to repair the Lord's temple. As they were making the repairs Hilkiah discovered a scroll with the Book of the Law. He brought this scroll to King Josiah and read it. When the King heard these words from the Lord, he tore his clothing in despair because he knew the people had disobeyed God's Law and he feared God's angry response. So King Josiah sent Hilkiah and several other men to go to Huldah to seek the Lord's advice.

Huldah knew that she had God's message for King Josiah and that it was not good news. Huldah confirmed that because the Jewish people had turned away from the Lord God that He was going to bring disaster on the city and the people because of their unfaithfulness. Yet everything Huldah had to say from the Lord wasn't all doom and gloom. She also had good news from the Lord.

Through Huldah, God told the messengers that He saw their sorrow and repentance after reading the Book of the Law. And, in fact, God would withhold His judgement and disaster until after King Josiah's death.

We don't know how Huldah felt having to give such dire news to such powerful men. Yet, as a prophet, she was committed to speaking God's truth to others whether it was well-received or ignored.

In your own faith community, do you see things which need to be adjusted? Do you move on in silence or do you take the courageous step to confront it?

Pivot from being fearful of what others will say when you speak of God's truth.

Pivot to keeping a clear conscience by speaking when you know you should and keeping quiet when that seems best.

Prayer

"Lord, thank You for this story of Huldah and her courage to speak Your truth to others. Help me to have the courage to live in Your ways each day. In the name of Jesus. Amen."

Your Pivotal Moment of Faith

Recall a time when you spoke courageously to a family member or co-worker about something that needed to change. How did you feel God at work then? Is there still more truth needed in those situations.

The Woman at the Well: Changed When She Met Jesus

"But whoever drinks the water I give them will never thirst. Indeed, the water I give them will become in them a spring of water welling up to eternal life." (John 4:14)

Throughout the Gospels and the three-year ministry of Jesus, none of His encounters were random. Jesus consistently spent time in prayer and His Heavenly Father directed His actions. On one occasion, told about in John 4, the disciples and Jesus were traveling and visited the region of Samaria. This was notable because the majority of Jews avoided Samaria. When they reached a place known as Jacob's well, His disciples walked to the nearby city of Sychar to buy some food. It was late in the day and a time when almost no one was at the well.

As Jesus watched, a Samaritan woman came to the well by herself to draw water. Jesus could tell right away that this woman was an outcast even among her own people. Most women would come to the well earlier in the day when it was cooler. There they could socialize as they drew water from the well. Jesus then broke custom and spoke directly to this Samaritan woman. "Will you give me a drink of water?"

With a confused look on her face, the woman said, "I'm a Samaritan woman and you are a Jew. Why are you asking me for a drink of water?"

Jesus answered, "If you knew who was talking with you, you could be asking me for living water?

"I don't understand," the woman said." You don't have anything to draw water from this well. Where can I get this living water that you are talking about?"

"If you drink regular water you will be thirsty again but everyone who drinks the living water from me will never be thirsty again."

The woman said, "Please give me some of this living water."

Jesus said, "Go call your husband and come back."

"I don't have a husband," she said.

"You have had five husbands but the man you are living with now is not your husband."

"You must be a prophet," the woman said with surprise that Jesus knew these details about her life. "And the Christ or Messiah is coming someday."

"I am the Messiah," Jesus said to her. The woman left her water jars and went into the village telling everyone that she had found the Messiah.

Whatever the woman had been expecting when she went to the well that day, her expectations were shattered by an encounter with the Messiah. In their brief conversation, she was able to see how only a relationship with Jesus could satisfy her needs forever. And just like that, this woman who had been scorned by so many people ran to tell others about the Messiah she had met. It takes courage to share your faith. As we cross paths with others, if we overcome our fear and take courage, we can engage anyone who crosses our path in a spiritual conversation.

Pivot from believing that the Words of hope that you know, and carry cannot have an impact on other souls God has put in your path.

Pivot to having more confidence that if God leads you to a hurting or bankrupt soul that He will both give you the heart to care and the words to share.

Prayer
"Lord, give me the courage in my everyday life to shine for You and engage people in spiritual discussions. Open these doors in my life. In the name of Jesus, amen."

Your Pivotal Moment of Faith
When was the last time you engaged someone in a spiritual conversation? If it's been a long time, write down at least one name of someone you have been hoping to have conversations about Jesus with.

Mary, The Woman Who Anointed Jesus: Serving in Humility

"Jesus said to the woman, 'Your faith has saved you; go in peace.'" (Luke 7:50)

One evening in Bethany, Simon, a Pharisee invited Jesus to come to his home for dinner. As they reclined and ate, an uninvited yet broken and sad woman, Mary, sat down near the feet of Jesus. She wet His dusty feet with her tears and wiped them clean with her hair. Next, she took an alabaster jar of perfume and coated His feet with the perfume. All four Gospels contain a description of this event. And while the accounts in Matthew 26, Mark 14, and Luke 7 do not name the woman, the account in John 12 identifies her as Mary, the sister of Lazarus.

As Mary touched Jesus, Simon thought to himself, "I thought Jesus was a prophet and if he were, he would know that this sinful woman is touching him."

The Son of God knew what Simon was thinking and said, "I have something to tell you. There was a moneylender and two people owed him money. One person owed 500 denarii and the other owed 50 denarii. He forgave the debt of both of them. Which of them will have the most love for the moneylender?"

Simon said, "Probably the person who had the larger forgiven debt."

"That is the correct answer," Jesus said. Then Jesus turned toward Mary and said, "Do you see this woman? When I entered your house, you didn't give me any water to wash my feet. yet with her tears, Mary wet my feet then dried them with her hair. You did not give me a kiss, but she has not stopped kissing my feet. You didn't put oil on my head but Mary poured expensive perfume on my feet. While her sins are many, because of her great love, they are forgiven."

Then Jesus spoke to Mary, "Your sins are forgiven." Jesus knew other guests were wondering how Jesus could forgive sins. And Jesus added to Mary, "Your faith has saved you. Go in peace."

The Pharisees were known for their outward and ritual observance of religious practices. Through His teaching, Jesus often criticized their outward practices like sitting in the best seats or saying loud prayers in public.

Instead of our outward actions, the Lord is concerned about the condition of our heart and mind. Mary, who anointed Jesus and His feet, didn't care about what anyone thought of the appearance. She was acting from the passion in her heart. As a result of her beautiful actions towards Jesus that showed where her heart truly was, her "great" sins were forgiven. It is the Holy Spirit which lives inside our hearts as Christians and directs our thoughts and our actions.

Pivot from believing that an outwards appearance of goodness is what God wants most.

Pivot to knowing that it's the actions of the heart that Jesus is most impressed with; actions that come from humility and serving others without anything to gain.

Prayer
"Father, thank You for this example of Mary and her tender actions of love to Jesus Christ. May we learn how to have the same faith to express our love to others in our family, our workplace and our neighborhood. In the name of Jesus, amen."

Your Pivotal Moment of Faith
How do Mary's love-filled actions toward Jesus inspire you to love others? Write down several practical actions you will take during this next week to show your love toward others.

Joseph: Forgiveness Instead of Revenge

"'For if you forgive other people when they sin against you, your heavenly Father will also forgive you. But if you do not forgive others their sins, your Father will not forgive your sins.'"
(Matthew 6:14-15)

Famine swept through the land of Canaan and Jacob, heard that Egypt still had grain. Jacob said to his sons, "Why do you continue to sit and look at each other? I've heard Egypt has grain. Go down and buy some of it so we can live and not starve." (See Genesis 42:1-2)

Ten of the brothers, without the youngest Benjamin, were sent to Egypt to purchase grain. When the brothers arrived in Egypt, they stood in a line to make the purchase. The Governor of Egypt was Joseph, but they didn't recognize him. The last time they had seen their brother, they had just sold him to slave merchants in a fit of jealousy.

What Joseph's brothers didn't know is that the merchants had sold Joseph to Potiphar where he prospered until Potiphar's wife tried to seduce him. She falsely accused Joseph of seducing her and he was thrown into prison. The head of the prison put Joseph in charge until he interpreted the dreams of one of Pharoah's servants and was brought to the attention of Pharoah. God's hand was on

Joseph, and he became second in command of the country. So much had changed about him that when his brothers arrived to purchase grain, they bowed down and did not recognize him. But Joseph recognized them.

Deciding to test his brothers, Joseph said, "You are spies and have come to see where our land is unprotected."

The brothers protested saying they were not spies but all sons of one man from Canaan. They told the unrelenting governor of their father and their youngest brother, Benjamin, back home. And they also mentioned the one son their father had lost.

Joseph insisted, "You are spies and I will throw you into prison." After three days he released them but demanded they return with their youngest brother. When the brothers talked among themselves in Hebrew, they said, "We are being punished because of what we did to Joseph." They didn't know Joseph could understand them. He turned away and wept until he could control his emotions. Then Joseph bound Simeon and sent the rest home with their grain. Joseph also commanded that their money be returned and packed in with the grain.

After several months they had gone through the grain they had carried from Egypt, and so they needed to return to Egypt for more. The brothers talked Jacob into releasing Benjamin into their care for the trip and took their original silver and more silver to purchase their grain. The brothers humbly returned to Egypt and Joseph invited them to his home and sat them in the order of their birth.

While the brothers didn't recognize Joseph, ultimately, he revealed himself to them. Instead of seeking revenge for selling them into slavery, Joseph tells his brothers, "The Lord guided my life and gave me this position to protect our family." Then Joseph explained the famine would continue for several years. It would be best if everyone including his father moved to Egypt. As Joseph said in Genesis 45:7, "But God sent me ahead of you to preserve for you a remnant on earth and to save your lives by a great deliverance."

The wisdom God gave Joseph while he endured is what helped save an entire nation. Some wisdom only comes through intense pressure.

Pivot from the notion that bad things that happen in life can't serve us—or others.

Pivot to not overreacting when bad happens, but instead trust that God can work all things together for good, for those who love Him and are called according His purpose (Romans 8:38).

Prayer
"Lord, thank You for the spiritual insight You gave Joseph about his life journey and how You led him through each situation. Please guide my life and provide direction for the large and small decisions I make. I am grateful for Your Presence. In the name of Jesus, amen."

Your Pivotal Moment of Faith
As the Lord guided Joseph, He also guides our lives. Pause in prayer and gratitude.

Cornelius: Life-Changing Prayer

"Therefore confess your sins to each other and pray for each other so that you may be healed. The prayer of a righteous person is powerful and effective." (James 5:16)

One of the most dramatic shifts in the New Testament came with the story of a devout Roman centurion named Cornelius. He was known for his generosity, fearing God and continued prayers. Acts 10 tells us all about him.

One day in a vision during prayer, Cornelius saw an angel who said, "Your prayers have been answered. Now send men to Joppa to Peter who is staying in the home of Simon, the Tanner. Peter will tell you what you should do."

Cornileus called two of his household servants and one of his soldiers and sent them to Joppa for Peter. While these three servants were traveling, Peter went up to the roof to pray and became hungry. In a vision, Peter saw the heavens open. Then a sheet came down filled with all types of four-footed animals, reptiles and birds which were unclean animals. As he watched the sheet, Peter heard a voice which commanded, "Peter, rise kill and eat."

"But Lord," Peter objected, "Throughout my life I have never eaten anything unclean or common."

In the vision, Peter heard, "Whatever God has cleaned, you can't call common." For three times on the rooftop, Peter watched this vision with the sheet and the unclean animals. Just as it was over, Peter began to think about what the vision meant. Then the three men from Cornelius arrived at Simon's door and asked for Peter. The Spirit said to Peter's heart, "Go with these men and doubt nothing for I have sent them."

Peter left with the men for the home of Cornelius. The next day, they arrived at Cornelius' home where he had gathered some people. The Centurion immediately bowed down to Peter, but Peter asked him to stand and not bow. Cornelius explained about the angel who sent the men to Peter. The meaning of his vision was clear to Peter. This disciple of Jesus proclaimed Jesus Christ was Lord of all and not just for the Jewish people. As Peter spoke, Cornelius and others in the group began to speak in tongues and God's spirit poured on these Gentiles, just like on the Day of Pentecost. In the name of Jesus, Peter baptized them and stayed with them for a few days.

The dramatic story of Peter and Cornelius shows the beginning of the spread of the Good News beyond the Jews . . . to Gentiles. This story also teaches us the powerful guidance from God when we have a life committed to prayer and service, like Cornelius.

Pivot from any type of belief that some are beyond God's amazing grace and forgiveness.

Pivot to total acceptance that each person, each soul, has immeasurable value to God, and so then, to us.

Prayer

"God, thank You that the Good News about Jesus is for every person in the world. We are thankful for this story of how You led Peter and Cornelius. Use it to convict our hearts to love others, and to spend more time in prayer. In Your name. Amen."

Your Pivotal Moment of Faith

Examine your list of friends in your life. What three steps could you take to expand your friendships to include those not like you?

Tabitha: God's Care for Widows

"Religion that God our Father accepts as pure and faultless is this: to look after orphans and widows in their distress and to keep oneself from being polluted by the world." (James 1:27)

During the early days of the church, some of the stories about believers are captured in the Acts of the Apostles. In Acts 9 we read about Tabitha (known as Dorcas in Greek) who was a disciple known for her charity and good works. Sadly, she became sick and died. Her friends prepared her body and laid her in an upper room. But when the disciples heard Peter was nearby a couple of them were sent to bring Peter to Tabitha.

Without delay, Peter came with them to that upper room where Tabitha was laying. A number of widows were weeping in the room and showed Peter the tunics and cloaks Tabitha had made. "Will everyone please leave this room?" Peter asked. As Peter knelt next to the body of this devoted disciple, did he remember Jairus? Several years earlier, Peter along with James and John, were with Jesus going to the house of Jairus, the synagogue leader. His daughter had died. Jesus sent the weeping people out of the room. To her mother and father along with the three disciples, Jesus explained the girl was only sleeping. Then the Lord picked up her hand and told her to get up.

The three disciples witnessed the power of God raise a person from the dead.

Now in Joppa standing next to Tabitha, Peter got on his knees and began to pray. After a while Peter turned toward the woman and said, "Tabitha, get up." She opened her eyes and when she saw Peter, she sat up and put her hand into his hand.

Peter helped Tabitha up and called her friends back into the room. The news of this miracle spread throughout the city and many people put their faith and trust in Jesus because of this miracle.

As believers, James tells us to look after orphans and widows. Raising the widow Tabitha from the dead was a miracle which encouraged the believers in Joppa and spread the Good News about Jesus. Where in your life are there widows that you can help and touch with the Good News about Jesus? This ministry can be a part of our walk of faith and a way we spread the light of Jesus into our community.

Pivot from ignorance and indifference to the needs of the vulnerable around you.

Pivot to finding ways to support those in your life who could use a little extra help.

Prayer

"Lord, thank You for caring about the widows and orphans in our world. Lead me and show me what You want me to do in this area of ministry. In the name of Jesus. Amen."

Your Pivotal Moment of Faith

Take some action to reach out to a widow or orphan in your church or community. Or search for a ministry online that works with widows and orphans to learn volunteer opportunities that are available.

Rebekah: Following the Lord in Faith

"Now faith is confidence in what we hope for and assurance about what we do not see. This is what the ancients were commended for."
(Hebrews 11:1-2)

Where could Abraham find the right wife for his son Issac? At 160 years of age, Abraham's greatest concern was to locate the right bride for his son Isaac. In Genesis 24 we read that Abraham sent for his oldest and trusted servant who swore that he would go back to the land of Abraham's family and search for Isaac's bride. In addition, this servant promised not to take Isaac back to his homeland. The son would remain in Canaan. Abraham, said, "God will send his angel to guide you and if the woman is unwilling to return with you, you will be released from your oath but do not take my son to that land."

When the servant arrived in the land in the evening, he prayed that the appointed woman would give him a drink and also water his camels. Before he finished praying a beautiful girl named Rebekah came and watered his camels. When he asked more about her and her family, the servant discovered that she was part of Abraham's extended family. In other words, she was exactly the relative he was looking for. The servant brought out various gifts that he brought for Isaac's bride.

Then he asked if her family had room to lodge him and his animals.

Rebekah took the servant and introduced him to her brother who was named Laban. The servant told of his mission to find a bride for Abraham's son and of how he had prayed for guidance and of how Rebekah was an answer to his prayer. After hearing the story, her brother, Laban and her father, Bethuel said, "The Lord has spoken." The servant praised God and gave the family additional gifts.

His mission accomplished, the servant wanted to return to Abraham with Rebekah the very next day. The family objected and wanted a few more days with Rebekah. But when they asked Rebekah, she replied "I will go." With such a simple response, her life was changed forever.

The next morning, they began the return journey. As they were nearing the place where Abraham lived, Isaac saw them from a distance and took off to welcome them.

Isaac and Rebekah were soon married.

When Rebekah and her family heard the story of Abraham's servant and about how God had answered his prayers, it was obvious to everyone that God was in this momentous event (Genesis 24:50). And even though Rebekah had no idea what was awaiting her at the other end of her journey back to Isaac, her husband-to-be, she at least left confident in the knowledge that God was guiding her steps. Our own life of faith often involves going in directions where we can't see the end of the journey. But walking faithfully with God Day by day, we can be confident that when he leads us into the unknown, he walks besides us every step of the way. As believers, "We live by faith, not by sight" (2 Corinthians 5:7).

Pivot from never involving God in your most important decisions.

Pivot to a faith that knows God is fully able to lead you in the directions that are right for you.

Prayer
"Father, the life of faith as a believer is challenging. Guide my steps and my decisions today as You guided Rebekah in the days of the old. In Jesus' name, Amen."

Your Pivotal Moment of Faith
Consider a decision you will make today. Take the first step of faith in your journey and trust God to guide the ending,

Deborah: A Role Outside of the Norm

"Since you are my rock and my fortress, for the sake of your name lead and guide me."
(Psalm 31:3)

After the death of Joshua, who led the nation of Israel after Moses, a series of men became judges to guide the people. But in general, this was a dark period of history for the nation of Israel. Throughout the book of Judges, we see a vicious cycle repeated: Israel falls into sin; foreign oppressors move in; Israel calls out for deliverance; God sends a judge to save Israel; Israel falls into sin..."

For the most part, the judges of Isreal were men. Deborah was the sole exception, and we meet her in Judges 4. As a woman and wife with exceptional integrity and a deep devotion to God, Deborah received revelation from the Lord for the people and negotiated conflicts among them. Yet during her years as a judge, the Israelite people continued to spiral downward into political unrest, moral depravity, and spiritual blindness. As the people fell into evil and depravity, God turned them over to Canaanite King Jabin and his commander Sisera who oppressed the people with cruelty for twenty years.

The Lord gave Deborah a revelation that they would be released from King Jabin. She sent for Barak and told him, "The God of Israel, commands you: 'Go, take with you 10,000 men of Naphtali and Zebulun. When you lead them up to Mount Tabor, I will draw Sisera, the commander of Jabin's army, with his chariots and his troops to the Kishon River and give him into your hands.'"

Barak listened to her directions and said to Deborah, "If you go with me, I will go; but if you don't go with me, I won't go."

Deborah agreed to go with Barak but then spoke this prophecy "but because of the course you are taking, the honor will not be yours for the LORD will deliver Sisera into the hands of a woman" (Judges 4:9).

Barak pursued Sisera's troops, and they were killed and the commander Sisera fled from the battle. Another woman is introduced into the story here. Sisera fled on foot to the tent of Jael, the wife of Heber the Kenite, because there was an alliance between Jabin king of Hazor and the family of Heber the Kenite.

"Come right in, my Lord. Don't be afraid" Jael said to Sisera. The commander entered her tent, and she covered him with a blanket and gave him a drink. Exhausted Sisera fell into a deep sleep. Seizing the opportunity, Jael picked up a tent peg and a hammer and killed him.

And so Deborah's prophetic words about the battle came true. "'Hear this, you kings! Listen, you rulers! I, even I, will sing to the LORD; I will praise the LORD, the God of Israel, in song" (Judges 5:3). The people had freedom for the next forty years.

As in the time of the Judges, we need some God-driven leaders to stand boldly for God. . Deborah was an unexpected leader. Perhaps you're an unexpected leader, as well.

Pivot from thinking you've no value in the Kingdom of God.

Pivot to being open to start the process of learning how to use the gifts God has given you in ways great or small.

Prayer
"Lord, guide our leaders and guide me in Your service even if it means taking on challenges I might think impossible today. Open doors that no man can shut in my life. In the name of Jesus. Amen."

Your Pivotal Moment of Faith
Where might the Lord be calling you to lead? Be open to His direction in your life.

The Bleeding Woman: Desperate to Touch Jesus

"'Therefore, I tell you, whatever you ask for in prayer, believe that you have received it, and it will be yours.'" (Mark 11:24)

The crowds around Jesus increased as the Lord healed people and drove out demons. Even one of the synagogue leaders, Jarius, pleaded with Jesus to heal his ill daughter. Jesus agreed to go with this worried father and many others in the crowd also continued down the street. The people were clamoring for Jesus' attention, but one woman was especially anxious to get to Jesus.

The Gospels of Matthew, Mark, and Luke tell us of this woman. She is described as "a woman...who had been subject to bleeding for twelve years." The woman had turned to many different types of doctors, yet none of them had healed her bleeding. And now, out of money, she had one last hope.

Seeing the crowds gathering around Jesus she woman thought, "if I can only touch the hem of His robe I will be healed." As Jesus drew near, she mustered her strength and pushed thorough the crowds and came up behind Jesus walking with Jairus. Reaching out, her fingers rested on Jesus' cloak. Instantly she knew that her bleeding had stopped. She was healed and freed from her suffering.

Jesus stopped. He had sensed the healing power go out and asked who had touched Him. It seemed a ridiculous question in the throng, but Jesus continued scanning the crowd. The woman quaked in fear as she watched Jesus' eyes move from one person to the next. Not knowing what to expect, but knowing she had been healed, the woman fell at Jesus' feet and told him everything.

With eyes filled with love and compassion, Jesus said, "'Daughter, your faith has healed you. Go in peace and be freed from your suffering'" (Mark 5:34). How the woman's heart must have soared to hear those words!

Imagine if that woman had chosen to stay home that day. Imagine if she had decided that the crowds were too much. Imagine if she had pulled back at the last minute thinking it was silly to expect to be healed by touching someone's cloak. Sometimes faith is the logical choice, but so often faith takes us beyond our reasoning. But over and again, the message of the Bible is that faith in God is faith that will be amply rewarded.

Pivot from only relying solely on your own reasoning to plan your future.

Pivot to allowing God to surprise you with the plans He has for your life.

Prayer
"God, thank You for Your healing of this woman who touched the robe of Jesus. Increase my faith as I live for You day in and day out. I need Your

touch through Your Holy Spirit. In Jesus' name. Amen."

Your Pivotal Moment of Faith

What steps of faith can you take with your family? How can you follow His lead in your workplace or community to increase your faith and trust of Him.

Matthew: He Counted the Cost

"I have not come to call the righteous, but sinners to repentance." (Luke 5:32)

Among the Jews in Israel during the earthly ministry of Jesus, one profession was universally despised: tax collectors, also known as publicans. They were typically Jewish but were not men of high character who had normal religious roots. The Romans did not care if they collected more tax than needed, they just wanted their quota. Naturally, if they had friends, they were the unsavory types that most Jews would have considered "unclean." They were true outcasts, though rich ones.

Jesus saw Matthew sitting at the tax collector's booth and said, "Follow me." Matthew must have had his mind already made up from he'd heard himself or others, as he got up and followed Him. While Jesus was having dinner at Matthew's house, many tax collectors and sinners came and ate with Him and His disciples. When the religious leaders and the Pharisees saw where Jesus was having dinner, they asked His disciples, "Why does your teacher eat with tax collectors and sinners?"

When He heard the question to His disciples Jesus said, "It is not the healthy who need a doctor, but the sick. But go and learn what this means: 'I desire mercy, not sacrifice.' For I have not come to call the righteous, but sinners" (Matthew 9:12-13).

These must have been words that were music to Matthew's ears. He'd just made the biggest decision of his life, leaving a profession that made him rich, but unloved. Now he was unemployed—and still unloved and untrusted by the normal people—except he found acceptance and love from Jesus.

As the familiar phrase goes, he chose "wisely."

There was a real cost to his choice, a cost that many have faced over the centuries. Yet he made it with courage. The result? As one of the twelve disciples, Matthew got to write his Gospel for Jewish followers of Jesus—many of whom likely had hurled scathing insults at him before—and after—his encounter with the Savior! Through his stories about the life of Jesus, Matthew wanted to convince his fellow Jews that Jesus was truly the Messiah whose kingdom had been fulfilled in a spiritual manner. In detail, Matthew explained how Jesus fulfills the teachings of the prophets in the Old Testament. He wrote beautifully about normal Christian character when he compiled the Beatitudes in Matthew 5 through 7. He shared countless parables about the Kingdom, and he spoke of the end of the age. Finally, he ended his Gospel with the challenge that has echoed through history: "Go ye therefore and make disciples…"

Pivot from believing that following Jesus comes without cost.

Pivot to understanding the cost of following Jesus and being able to explain some of these costs to those you are trying to reach for Christ.

Prayer

"God thank You for the example of Matthew leaving a life of wealth and prosperity to follow the teaching of Jesus. Help me to learn these lessons and incorporate them into my daily life. In Jesus' name, amen."

Your Pivotal Moment of Faith

Matthew made a pivotal decision to leave the wealth of his work and follow Jesus. How has following Jesus changed your life? Take a moment and write a few sentences expressing your gratitude towards Jesus.

Saul Becomes Paul: Meeting Jesus Face to Face

"But rejoice inasmuch as you participate in the sufferings of Christ, so that you may be overjoyed when his glory is revealed. If you are insulted because of the name of Christ, you are blessed, for the Spirit of glory and of God rests on you."
(1 Peter 4:13-14)

After the resurrection of Jesus, the early Christians were a threat to the religious order of the Jewish leaders. Saul of Tarsus was schooled as a Pharisee and got caught up with the other leaders in the synagogue who were against anything related to this new movement. When the disciple Stephen was dragged before the leaders and defended his faith, the leaders decided to stone Stephen. When they dragged him out of the city and began stoning him, Saul stood nearby observing.

Acts 9 picks up the story. Saul soon headed to Damascus with some other men to gather and punish more Christians. While on the road, a blinding light from heaven surrounded Saul. He fell to the ground as he heard, "Saul, why are you persecuting me?"

Confused as to what was happening, Saul said, "Who are you, my Lord?"

"I am Jesus, who you are persecuting. Now get up and go into the city and you will be told what to do next."

Suddenly, Saul was blind. Standing there in the road in broad daylight, the world went dark. His friends had to guide him into the city where he stayed for three days. Saul did not eat or drink but spent his time in prayer.

One day a disciple Ananias came to Saul, saying, "'Brother Saul, the Lord—Jesus, who appeared to you on the road as you were coming here—has sent me so that you may see again and be filled with he Holy Spirit.' Immediately, something like scales fell from Saul's eyes, and he could see again. He got up and was baptized" (Acts 9:17-18). Saul ate and drank to restore his strength and then spent a number of days in the city with the disciples there.

After several days, Saul went to the local synagogue and proclaimed that Jesus Christ was the Lord. His preaching confused some of the people saying, "Isn't this the man who has persecuted Christians in Jerusalem. I thought he brought letters from the chief priests to round up Christians?" After many days the local Jews plotted to kill Saul, but he learned about their plot and escaped. They lowered him down the Damascus wall in a basket.

This change in direction for Saul of Tarsus is one of the most dramatic conversions in the New Testament. Saul changed his name to Paul and became the Apostle to the Gentiles, writing many letters in the New Testament. His testimony can give us an idea how we can tell our story of a changed life.

Pivot from thinking you have to be a scholar or a person with degrees to share the message of faith in Christ.

Pivot to focusing on your story and how Christ has changed you. Allow God to work in their heart as you share your testimony of God's faithfulness.

Prayer
"Lord, thank You for the change in Paul's life on the road to Damascus. Help me to celebrate Paul's story and also to tell my own story of a transformed life."

Your Pivotal Moment of Faith
Take some time to write your own testimony. Then choose several people to tell about how God has changed your life.

About Back to the Bible

Back to the Bible was founded in 1939 by Bible teacher Theodore Epp. For many decades, the Back to the Bible radio broadcast was heard across the nation and even overseas. Featuring speakers like Woodrow Kroll, and Warren Wiersbe, Back to the Bible became known for its solid Bible teaching.

Times change of course. And with the rise of the Internet came new challenges and opportunities. Heading into the 21st century Back to the Bible began shifting to a personalized message delivery strategy and learner-centered design. No longer would only one message be delivered to all people. Instead, each user could receive a daily spiritual fitness workout from God's Word tailored to their specific needs—delivered through the GOtandem smartphone app and web-based platform.

This high level of customization is driven by Back to the Bible's Spiritual Fitness CheckUP. This short assessment asks the user how they are doing spiritually and delivers immediate recommendations of Scripture passages and teaching for their spiritual struggles or desired areas of growth. It is also an introduction to the daily spiritual fitness workout process that is available. Users regularly share how they overcome temptation, defeat struggles, or increase their knowledge of the Bible.

To help believers develop a daily habit of growing closer to Jesus and bringing Him to others, the

Center for Spiritual Fitness (CSF) was created as a Christian research center that provides social science data and theological insights to help contemporary Christians maintain their spiritual fitness in an increasingly secular world. The CSF also helps direct our content creation departments with insight into needs and upcoming trends.

It was through the efforts of the CSF that we discovered our revolutionary 4-Step Methodology. We know through our research that when an individual Reads the Word of God, takes time to Reflect on its meaning, respond by putting the Bible's teaching into practice, and, finally, Reveal these truths to others, they will grow closer to Jesus and fulfill His mission of reaching the world with the Gospel.

And now in 2025, though we are using technology our founder could scarcely imagine, our mission remains the same: To teach the Bible. More than just a Bible delivery ministry, Back to the Bible is committed to walking with you to help you grow stronger spiritually.

Visit our website at backtothebible.org to find out more and to get started with your own Spiritual Fitness CheckUP!

For more information about Back to the Bible, the GOtandem app, or the Center for Spiritual Fitness reach out to us at:

support@backtothebible.org
402-464-7200

About Arnie Cole

Arnie Cole (EdD, Pepperdine) is the CEO of Back to the Bible and Director of Research and Development for the *Center for Spiritual Fitness*. With his passion for research that helps people conquer their needs, Dr. Cole has been active most of his professional life in developing methodologies and best practices to instill significant behavioral change in individuals. A serial entrepreneur, Arnie pioneered disruptive organizations in California that successfully moved violent patients with developmental disabilities out of institutions and safely into the community and employment. Today he is responsible for the digital media ministries as well as Research & Development at Back to the Bible.

For the past 20 years, he has focused on research and field work into the spiritual lives of people around the world in their spiritual formation. From this, his teams have developed assessments that support needs-based algorithms at the heart of daily spiritual fitness apps and platforms. The goal is to help people engage in Scripture to find Romans 12:2 transformation and to activate mature Christ Followers in sharing their faith.

Dr. Cole is the co-author of several books, including *Unstuck: Your Life, God's Design, Real Change; Worry Free Living; Tempted, Tested, and True* (all Bethany House Publishers). Dr. Cole has also served with YWAM's Business as Missions group in the Middle East, CEO of MegaVoice LLC, as well as Vice President of Development for Mission Aviation Fellowship. Arnie and his wife Char are the parents of adult children and have 5 grandchildren. They operate Still Waters Equestrian Academy—a ministry sharing God's gift of horses as a community outreach. The Coles live near Lincoln, Nebraska.

www.ingramcontent.com/pod-product-compliance
Lightning Source LLC
Chambersburg PA
CBHW070531090426
42735CB00013B/2941